Self-Sufficiency
Grow Your Own
Fruits and Vegetables

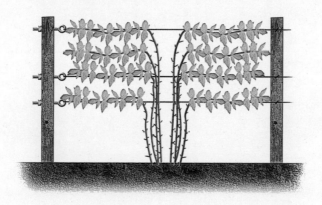

Self-Sufficiency

Grow Your Own

Fruits and Vegetables

Ian Cooke

Skyhorse Publishing

Skyhorse Publishing books may be purchased in bulk at special discounts for sales promotion, corporate gifts, fund-raising, or educational purposes. Special editions can also be created to specifications. For details, contact the Special Sales Department, Skyhorse Publishing, 307 West 36th Street, 11th Floor, New York, NY 10018 or info@skyhorsepublishing.com.

Skyhorse® and Skyhorse Publishing® are registered trademarks of Skyhorse Publishing, Inc.®, a Delaware corporation.

www.skyhorsepublishing.com

10 9 8 7 6 5 4 3 2 1

Library of Congress Cataloging-in-Publication Data is available on file.

ISBN: 978-1-61608-410-3

Printed in China

Note:
The author and publishers have made every effort to ensure that all information given in this book is safe and accurate, but they cannot accept liability for any resulting loss or damage to either property or person, whether direct or consequential or however arising.

CONTENTS

INTRODUCTION

Whether you're sure you want to grow your own fruit and vegetables and need some basic advice or you're still debating whether this is a valid exercise, this book will be helpful in advising and guiding on the basics of successfully growing most of the common fruits and vegetables.

To be truly self-sufficient for fruit and vegetables, you would need to be able to produce enough for consumption 365 days of the year. For most people this is unlikely to be feasible. Many people, however, may wish to become self-sufficient for some aspect of their food production, maybe basic vegetables for the year, salads for the summer, or just soft fruits.

Growing fruit and vegetables is not difficult providing you observe some basic techniques and carry out the different tasks at the right time. It does require commitment, however, particularly during the summer months, when weeds are growing rapidly and your vegetables and crops require harvesting almost daily. It can be time-consuming and it's not easy to take a break without your crops spoiling. It is better, therefore, to aim low initially, starting with a small plot and seeing how successful this is before you take on a full allotment.

There are many advantages to growing your own fruit and vegetables. Initially, whatever you grow can be harvested, prepared, cooked, if appropriate, and on your table within an hour or so. When you grow your own produce, you can also harvest at the ideal stage, so you can have small, tender young broad beans, finger-sized courgettes, and French beans as thin as pencils. And, of course, taste goes hand-in-hand with freshness. Such freshness and flavor can rarely be replicated from shop-purchased produce. Also, apart from the health benefits of increasing the amount of fruits and vegetables in your diet, the actual process of regularly tending a plot is good exercise.

When you grow your own, you can also choose the varieties that you wish to eat. Although you will want a good crop, I would suggest that in your own plot flavor should be a high priority. You can also choose to grow varieties of vegetable that aren't commercially widely available. For example, golden beet is an easily grown variation of beetroot that makes a delicious vegetable, but is rarely offered in the shops. French beans are available as tasty golden or curious purple types. There is also an increasing interest in heritage or heirloom varieties, as they are sometimes called. Old varieties of tomato and potato can have both a fascinating appearance and distinctive flavors.

Produce that has been picked from your own garden will also not have been contaminated with any pesticides or additives that you have not chosen to use. Although a lot of crops are now grown organically, many are not and will have been treated with pesticides, and subject to post-harvest treatments to prevent decay during the sales period. When you grow produce yourself, you know exactly what has been used. If you want to avoid using pesticides, you will need to follow various alternative ways of combating pests and diseases (see pages 36–49). In particular you can choose varieties that have inbred resistance.

So, is it financially viable? Initially there will be some expenditure on tools and basic equipment, plus there will be the annual costs of seeds, manures and fertilizers. A good investment always results in good yields, so buy quality seed and ensure that the soil is properly fertilised to start with. In most cases you will harvest crops valued far in excess of the costs of your initial seeds and fertilizers.

Now you've decided to give it a go, you can get started. The first three sections of this book will guide you through the basics of planning, soils, fertilizers, cultivation, pests, and diseases that are common ground for most production. The following three chapters look in detail at vegetable and fruit crops and using a greenhouse. If you are impatient to get going, however, the "Quickstart Guide" on page 10 may be just what you need.

Getting started

"There is no time like the present" is a familiar challenge, but the best time to start with fruit and vegetables is late winter or early spring; enough time to plant fruit trees and bushes and get soil cultivations complete ready for spring sowing. Garden centers will offer plenty of seeds and plants and you will soon see the results of your work.

Quickstart guide

Maybe you are so keen to get started that you don't have time to read the whole book before getting going. Well this is the page for you! Here are some suggestions for how you can immediately start with a few fast-growing and rewarding crops. References are to pages containing more detailed information on each point.

✷ Dig over the soil you want to use, removing all weeds (see pages 26–28).
✷ Tread lightly to firm the ground, rake it, and apply a general fertilizer at 60g/m^2 (2 oz./square yard) (see page 32–34).
✷ In early spring, sow seeds of lettuce, spring onions, and leaf radish (see pages 77–79) and carrots (see pages 66–67).
✷ Follow in late spring with French beans (see page 62), beetroot (see page 70), and spinach (see pages 85–86).
✷ Sow seeds thinly in rows 30 cm. (12 in.) apart (see page 56).
✷ Plant a few seed potatoes in a little soil in a deep pot or plastic drum and top up with soil as growth develops (see pages 71–73).
✷ In early summer look for plants of tomatoes, zucchinis, and sweetcorn in your local garden center and plant at about 45 cm. (18 in.) apart (see page 82).
✷ For a quick fruit crop, look in your garden center for some part-grown strawberry plants. Grow them in large pots to keep them away from slugs (see pages 100–102).
✷ Keep your crops well watered in dry conditions (see page 30).
✷ Harvest as soon as crops are big enough and re-sow the same crop for continuity.

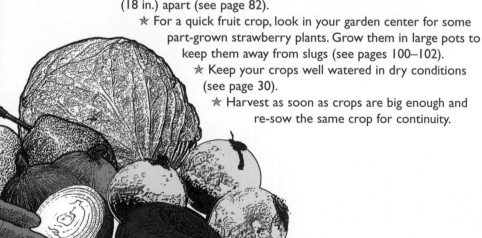

Where to grow fruit and vegetables

If you have space in your own back garden, then this is probably the best place for a kitchen garden. It's quick and easy to tend to your crops at regular intervals and convenient to pop out and harvest something fresh for a meal. You will also have access to water and, if needed, electricity and secure storage for your tools. If you don't have enough space in your own garden it may be that a neighbor has more garden than they need and may be willing to loan a section for your use. Usually a basket of vegetables on occasion is all they will want in recompense.

Allotments

Allotments may seem the next obvious choice. You will find yourself amongst a community of keen gardeners, probably with a wealth of experience, advice, and often friendly camaraderie. Some allotment sites are sophisticated but others are quite basic, so you need to check the facilities available. Some sites allow sheds and greenhouses whereas others don't. With the current popularity of growing vegetables, unfortunately most allotment sites have a waiting list, usually of a number of years.

Well-used plots may have problems with infected soil and neglected plots with weeds. It may take a whole season to clear up the plot before it can be used. Speak to existing allotment holders about problems and challenges, including pests and crime. A full-size allotment will enable you to grow almost anything you might want but will take up a great deal of time—you may wish to share, or ask for a half-sized plot.

Community Gardens

Community gardens and city farms are local initiatives based around a piece of land, usually where crops are grown and small animals, such as chickens, may be kept. Community gardens are often a lot more neighborhood based than allotments, with groups of individuals working together to grow food. Plots may be small and the work shared. Sometimes the plots will be expressions of the background of the local population, with various ethnic crops being grown. Community gardens can be large and well organized or quite simply small patches of unused land. In some areas, giant builders' bags filled with soil have been used to turn an empty patch of derelict concrete from an eyesore into a productive and colorful area.

Growing vegetables in small spaces

Many people would like to grow fruit and vegetables but feel that the space they have is too restricted. Even in a tiny garden or on a balcony, however, you can produce some home-grown vegetables and fruits. With a restricted space, select compact varieties and those that are sometimes called "mini vegetables." Use close spacing and harvest the vegetables when small, following with successional sowings to get the most from your space. Use any soil you have, plus growbags, pots, and containers. Always use new growbags and replace the soil in pots every year, to avoid a build-up of disease and to get the maximum yield from a small space. Avoid crops which take a long time to mature, such as bulb onions and winter brassicas, and those that take up a lot of space, such as maincrop potatoes and zucchinis.

Carrots, turnips, and beetroot will quickly produce small tender roots. Choose the leek "armor" for harvesting when young. A range of salads and leafy crops, such as spinach, can be grown in a small space. Broccoli will produce small central heads at a close spacing but is probably not worth growing them on for the secondary crop. "Avalanche" is a good small cauliflower and "minicole" a reliable cabbage for close spacing. Tomatoes, peppers, and eggplants can easily be grown in pots or growbags. The small trailing cherry tomato known as "tumbler" is happy in a hanging basket.

Dwarf French beans can be grown in pots. Tall, climbing runner beans need to be planted in the soil but a wigwam of five canes and plants does not take up much space, and will yield several pickings over many weeks. Cucumbers can be grown up a trellis or over an arch.

Containers
Vegetables will grow in all sorts of pots or plastic containers as long as they are deep enough and have drainage holes in the bottom. Disused builders' bags make excellent small beds and plastic compost sacks make large pots, excellent for growing potatoes. Commercial growbags can be used for quick-growing vegetables but are too shallow for deep-rooted vegetables or long-term crops. They can be used for salads, dwarf French beans, stump-rooted carrots, beetroot, and tomatoes.

Most multi-purpose composts will be suitable for growing vegetables and can be used for several crops over a year but will need to be replaced each season. The used compost can go on the compost heap. For longer-term crops, use compost that also contains some soil.

Potato Pots

A small crop of potatoes can be grown in a large pot, a tub, or a special potato bag. Start with about 20 cm. (8 in.) of good potting compost in the bottom. Plant the potatoes and keep well watered. As they grow, top up the compost in stages, no more than 7.5 cm. (3 in.) at a time. At harvest time, just tip out the whole pot and separate the potatoes from the compost. Remember that potato roots must grow in the dark or they become green, so don't try using clear plastic drums.

Growing fruit in small spaces

Growing fruit in a small space is even more challenging but not impossible. Most fruits need to grow in the open ground, although some can be grown in large pots. Most fruits prefer a sunny location. If you have some space against a wall, trained fruit trees, such as cordon apples, fan-trained plums or espalier pears, can be grown. These are regularly prunedm and so kept within a restricted space. Always make sure with any of the top fruits (see Types of fruit, page 90), such as apple, pear, plum, or cherry, that you purchase young trees that have been grafted on a dwarf rootstock. The dwarf nectarine "nectarella" is suitable for pot culture and produces full-sized, sweet juicy fruits.

One possibility for small gardens is the concept of a "family" apple tree. Three or more varieties are grafted onto the same rootstock, grow and produce three types of fruit. It is essential with such a tree that the different varieties will pollinate each other and that they will grow at a similar rate to each other to keep the tree in balance. You can also get pears grafted as family trees.

Redcurrants, white currants, and gooseberries can all be grown as upright cordons and take up very little space. Blackcurrants grow in a different manner and are rather too spreading for a confined space. Raspberries also grow vertically; three or five canes can be planted around a central post. Strawberries are easily grown in growbags, pots, or even in hanging baskets. Growing strawberries in above ground containers keeps the fruit off the soil and away from slugs.

Tools and equipment

If I got something wrong, my father always said, "a bad workman blames his tools!" Whether or not it's true, a good gardener needs a combination of skills and the right tools to do the job. The essentials for all gardening are a spade, fork, rake, hoe, trowel, pruning shears, and a wheelbarrow. Handle the spades on display until you are comfortable with one. A fork is probably the second most useful tool, and is used for a myriad jobs. There are smaller-sized spades and forks available which are lighter and may be more suitable for those with less strength. The most useful rake is a standard steel-headed rake that can be used to break down soil, level, and create a tilth.

Hoes come in many different styles. The Dutch hoe is the most useful for simple weeding and it is used with a pushing action, while walking backwards. For vegetable growing, a draw hoe will be needed, partly for taking out drills for seeds and also for earthing up potatoes. Hoes with short handles, called onion hoes, are very useful for close work, such as thinning seedlings. A wheelbarrow is probably an essential for fruit and vegetable production. If transporting materials is an issue, there are also barrows with large wheels like balloons and also ones with two wheels, sometimes called garden carts.

A trowel is a small tool, but choose it carefully, selecting one that has a smooth handle that fits comfortably in the palm of your hand. A garden line will be needed for sowing seeds and positioning plants in straight rows, or you can use a length of wood. If you need to apply pesticides, you will need a sprayer. Pruning shears, possibly long-armed loppers, and a small pruning saw will be needed to prune fruit trees. A watering can is always useful and plastic ones will be the lightest and longest lasting. When buying a hosepipe, buy a good-quality reinforced hose that will not kink and a reel to wind it on.

You should always have a sturdy pair of gardening gloves to protect your hands when doing tough jobs. There is nothing clever about grubbing about in the soil with bare hands as some TV personalities do. Soil can easily contain pathogens, which cause infections, and there is always the risk of broken glass or rusty metal. Having spent a lifetime with dry, chapped gardening hands, I am also a fervent user of disposable vinyl gloves for all garden jobs. Use a good skin cream on your hands before and after a gardening session.

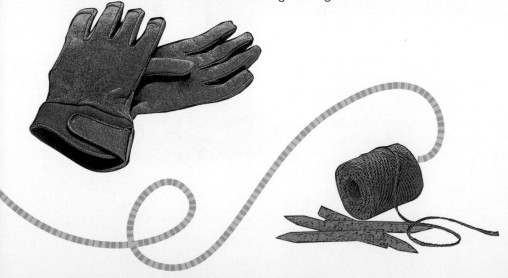

Harvesting and storage

Fresh fruit and vegetables are undoubtedly the tastiest and most nutritious but however hard you try to plan a succession of crops there will inevitably be some gluts. Some vegetables such as peas and sweetcorn all ripen at the same time, as do many fruits. Going on holiday or failing to harvest for a few days will also yield a bumper harvest. On a short-term basis most vegetables and fruit will store well in a cool pantry or refrigerator.

Most methods of long-term storage are kitchen techniques but some are horticultural procedures. Potatoes and onions will store well over winter in a cool, dry frost-free shed. Potatoes are best stored in thick paper sacks, not polythene. Onions are best tied together in a long string and hung from a shed roof. Apples and pears can be stored in open trays stacked up in a cool, frost free store. Ideally they should be wrapped individually in waxed paper to reduce moisture loss. Root crops such as potatoes, carrots, parsnips, and rutabagas can also be stored outdoors in a structure called a clamp. All stored fruit and vegetables should be checked regularly and any rotting specimens removed.

Moving to the kitchen, there are various other possibilities. Freezing is undoubtedly the easiest and most successful technique for a wide variety of both fruit and vegetables. Check a freezing guide for details on preparation and blanching times. Most fruits can be made into jams, and the traditional technique of bottling is quite successful with fleshy fruits such as pears and plums. Some vegetables, such as onions, red cabbage, and gherkins are suitable for pickling and others for making chutney. In particular, green tomatoes at the end of the season can be used to make a flavorsome winter pickle. Some beans can be allowed to fully ripen for drying in airtight jars. And, of course, most fruits, and indeed some vegetables, such as parsnips, can be used to produce very acceptable country wines.

The basics

Soil is the very basis from which plants grow. If you understand the basics of soils, how to cultivate them, and how to keep plants well fed and watered, then you are well on the way to producing fruit and vegetables. This chapter is all about these basics, which are the keys to almost any crops.

Soils for fruit and vegetables

Soil provides anchorage for plants and the essential source of moisture, air and nutrition. Topsoil is the rich, well-cultivated uppermost layer of soil, in which most plant roots grow. This is generally around 30 cm. (12 in.) deep, although it may vary considerably according to whether it has been well cultivated or neglected. Subsoil is the material below topsoil, which is generally poorer, more compacted, and less rich. By cultivating soil deeply and adding soil improvers, the depth of topsoil in a garden can be increased. This in turn will result in increased cropping potential.

A good soil will contain mineral solids, organic matter, air and water. The space for air and water is very important and when a soil is compacted, say with heavy wear or vehicles driving over it, the spaces for air and water are squashed out. This makes it much more difficult for plants to grow adequately. Cultivating a soil opens it up for air and water to penetrate.

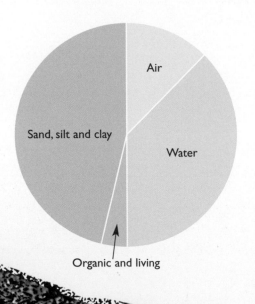

Air

Water

Sand, silt and clay

Organic and living

The mineral components of a soil are generally made up of three basic constituents: clay, silt, and sand. A good soil is one that contains a mixture of all three and gardeners call these soils loams. Medium loams are regarded as ideal soils, but not all gardeners are lucky enough to have soil of this type and you will have to learn to use the soil you have.

Clay soils

Clay soils are heavy and generally difficult to cultivate. They can be wet, poorly drained, and therefore often slow to warm up in the spring. They do, however, retain more moisture through the summer, are regarded as rich soils, and are good for fruit production. They can be improved with careful cultivation, organic matter, and possibly sharp sand.

Sandy and silty soils

Sandy soils are free draining, easy to cultivate, and tend to warm up quickly in the spring, making them good for vegetable production. In particular, root crops such as carrots will grow well. Sandy soils do not retain water or fertilizers well, so tend to need more irrigation in the summer and regular feeding. They, too, benefit from extra organic matter. Silty soils are not so common but are also good for growing vegetables. They generally behave more like sandy soils but are richer and less prone to drying out.

What's Your Soil?

Understanding the type of soil you have is important in knowing how to cultivate and what crops are likely to thrive. You can determine this by rubbing a small sample between your wetted fingers. A sandy soil is easy to ascertain as the sample feels rough and gritty and does not stick together. A clay soil feels sticky and a larger sample of it will actually roll into a shiny ball. Silty soils are more difficult to determine, but generally feel silky and smooth. With a loam you may be able to feel all the constituents in the mixture. Depending on the proportions, we may speak about having a sandy loam if the proportion of sand is high or a clay loam at the other end of the scale, and so on.

Soil pH

Soils can also be acidic or alkaline, and are measured on a scale called pH. In the middle of the scale at pH7, the soil is said to be neutral—neither acidic nor alkaline. Above pH7, soils are alkaline, and below, they are acidic. The ideal pH for many plants is pH6.5, just slightly acidic. Some plants are very sensitive to pH and will only grow at certain levels. For example, vegetables in the brassica family such as cabbages, Brussels sprouts, and turnips need a high pH to grow successfully. Contrastingly, potatoes prefer a slightly acidic soil. The availability of certain plant nutrients may also be controlled by pH.

The pH of a soil does not remain constant. The very action of rain and natural cycles within the soil slowly make it more acidic. From time to time it may be necessary to add lime or chalk to a soil to neutralize the acidity. Liming should be linked to crop rotation (see page 53) so that lime is applied just before a brassica crop is planted.

It is important to know the pH of the soil in your garden. Testing kits are readily available from garden centers. A small soil sample is taken from various areas and mixed together to give an average. The soil is then shaken up with a testing reagent and water in a small tube. The reagent changes color according to the pH and this can be checked against a color chart supplied with the kit.

A soil testing kit will usually also contain information on how much lime to use. Lime should ideally be added to the soil in the autumn as the response is slow and may not be fully effective until the next spring. It is difficult to reverse the effects of liming, so small quantities should be used and the effects monitored before adding more. Always wear rubber gloves, a dust mask, and eye protection when applying lime as it can be an irritant. Never apply lime at the same time as farmyard manure, as the two react, resulting in the release of excess ammonia, which will scorch roots and wastes the effect of both.

Life in the soil

A good soil is a living, thriving community all of its own. There are many small beneficial creatures, some visible, such as earthworms, wood lice, and centipedes, and others that include microscopic bacteria and fungi, which live within the soil and contribute to a healthy condition. One of the main activities of soil organisms is breaking down dead materials within the soil and converting them to organic matter. This is vitally important and adding extra organic matter is one of the best ways of improving almost any type of soil. There are many different sources of organic matter, but they are all derived from living materials.

Sources of Organic Matter

✳ Garden compost
✳ Recycled green waste (from your local authority)
✳ Farmyard manure
✳ Chicken manure
✳ Spent mushroom compost
✳ Leafmold
✳ Composted seaweed
✳ Spent hops or brewers' grains

All of these are valuable and vary in price according to whether there is a local source. Farmyard or chicken manure must be well rotted before use or it can damage the roots of plants. Mushroom compost is good, but is quite often alkaline, so should be linked to crops that need lime.

Gardening organically

Some gardeners may choose to produce crops on an organic basis, which means growing as naturally as possible, without the use of any chemical fertilizers, pesticides or weed killers. This is quite possible and, for many people, a matter of strong personal belief. All gardeners should respect wildlife within the garden and the living aspects of the soil in particular. For those who feel less strongly, a moderated approach using a mix of organic principles and modern fertilizers, together with a minimum of pesticides, is often an acceptable compromise.

Composting

Composting is a valuable process for all gardeners. A compost heap provides a means of disposing of the majority of your garden and kitchen waste, without having to send it to landfill. The end product is valuable for enriching the soil—it's a double winner! If at all possible, have two heaps. This enables you to have one rotting down, while you have another building up. Two heaps about the size of a cubic meter would be ideal for most small gardens. To keep it tidy, a compost heap is ideally made within a bin of some sort. Proprietary bins made of plastic are available from garden centers or in some areas are free from your local authority. Alternatively, a very usable bin can be made from old wooden pallets. Three sides will form a suitable enclosure; the fourth side needs to be loose or open, to give access.

Many different types of waste can be used in a compost heap. Some rough, loose material is useful at the bottom to keep the heap well drained. A good heap is made up of a mixture of materials. Some waste, such as cabbage stalks or prunings, can be quite woody, whereas fresh weeds or vegetable trimmings are soft and lush. Mixing various materials together helps the different types decompose. Small domestic shredders are now readily available and make it possible to process woody material, such as fruit prunings or tough cabbage stalks, into smaller components that will decompose more evenly and quickly.

Decomposition will not take place if the constituents are dry, so the heap should be watered if dry. Compost activators are available, which can be added to encourage the natural organisms to work, but these are not usually necessary if the heap is a good mixture of different ingredients. About six to eight weeks after the heap has been completed, "turn" the heap. Fork out the half-formed compost, mixing it up, letting fresh air into the heap, and stacking up again for the process to complete. This process is not essential but certainly helps in producing good compost in a short space of time.

Materials to Add to a Compost Heap

✴ Weeds
✴ Grass mowings
✴ Autumn leaves
✴ Dead plants and crops
✴ Dead flower heads or cut flowers
✴ Rootballs or used potting compost
✴ Vegetable peelings from the kitchen
✴ Tea leaves and coffee grounds
✴ Torn up newspaper
✴ Prunings and hedge trimmings (if shredded)

Avoid perennial weeds, diseased plants, pet feces, and cooked foods or meats, which will attract vermin.

A foul smell from a compost heap usually means that it is too wet, usually from too many lush materials, such as wet grass mowings. Shaking it out and adding drier materials will usually help to get it back on course. Compost is ready when it resembles a crumbly dark brown material, in which you can barely recognise the original constituents. It should smell earthy but not unpleasant. This may take between three to six months depending on the time of year.

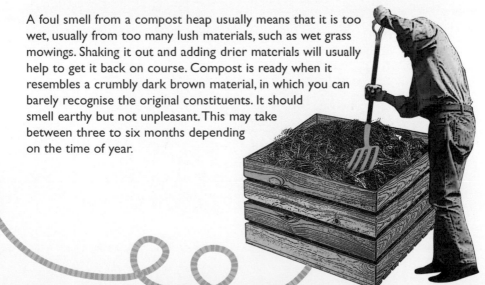

Soil cultivations

Soil cultivations are at the heart of most growing techniques, and particularly so with vegetable growing. These will include digging, forking, hoeing, and raking. You should avoid cultivating your soil when it is wet. This is particularly important for clay soils, which are sticky and can easily be damaged if cultivated wet. The most valuable technique is digging, which is the basis for preparing soils for almost any type of growing. The whole process improves drainage and aeration of the top layer of soil. Digging can be done at any time, although it is particularly valuable to dig clay soils before the winter, as cold, wind, and frost will help break up the surface and make it more friable for spring plantings.

Single digging

The basic method is single digging using a spade. To do this you should take out a small trench the width of the area to be cultivated and transport the surplus soil to the far end of the plot. Digging then proceeds, inverting the soil into the open trench, burying weeds and leaving a fresh layer of soil on the surface. You should work backwards to the end, where the surplus soil goes into the final trench. Compost or other organic matter can be added to the open trench before covering with soil. Lazy gardeners often avoid making a trench and digging in this situation becomes a muddle!

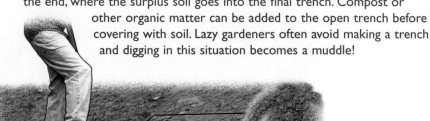

Double digging

Double digging is a traditional and laborious technique that breaks up the soil to twice a spade's depth. It is very valuable on land that is compacted or has not been previously cultivated. The process is started with a double width trench about 60 cm. (2 ft.) wide. The soil is taken out and moved to the end of the plot. The base of the trench is then broken up with a fork, down to another spit's depth. Organic matter can again be added before the topsoil is inverted into this trench, creating a second trench, and so on.

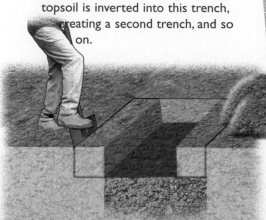

No Dig Garden

Sounds ideal! This is a technique whereby we give the soil minimum disturbance but apply a thick dressing of fresh garden compost each year and allow worms and other organisms to incorporate it into the soil. Your vegetables are sown directly into the new layer of compost. The basic soil must be well cultivated and free from any drainage problems before embarking on this technique, and it is essential not to compact the soil by walking on it. This, therefore, works best with small beds that can be tended from either side. The compost must be well-rotted and weed-free.

Using a rotavator

The use of a rotary cultivator to quickly cultivate large areas seems very attractive, particularly to those with limited time, and such machines can be very valuable but they do have problems. These are heavy pieces of equipment and handling them to cultivate a neglected plot can be hard, shoulder-wrenching work—not a job for the frail! Rotavators also smash through the soil and can quickly turn good soils into either dust or a sticky mess. They should only be used when the soil is moist but not wet.

Dealing with weeds

Cleaning up a plot infested with perennial weeds such as couch grass, ground elder, bindweed, and brambles is a tough job. Any woody growth such as the brambles and maybe small tree seedlings should be dug out and cleared away. Probably the most efficient and quickest way of dealing with perennial weeds is to use the herbicide glyphosate. This should be applied during the spring and summer months to weeds in full growth. It is absorbed by the weeds and kills the whole weed, including the roots. More than one application may be required for persistent weeds. This chemical is very safe to use, and once it touches the soil, is broken down to harmless components. You can also go ahead and sow or plant as soon as the weeds are dead. Beware, however—it will also kill any green plants you spray it on.

If you do not want to use chemicals, it is a slower job. The whole site can be covered with a sheet of thick black plastic or an old carpet. Weeds attempt to grow but, providing they cannot reach the light, will fail and die. Leave the covering in place for at least a full summer season and then dig over. If weeds appear after you start using the plot, the trick is to repeatedly hoe them off, which weakens them, causing eventual death. Avoid rotavating a plot that is infested with perennial weeds. The blades of a rotavator cut up the weeds and you will end up with many more.

Water in the soil

An adequate supply of water is essential for healthy plant growth. A good, well-structured soil will have plenty of open spaces within it, which not only allow for air to penetrate but are also capable of absorbing water. Good soils act as a sponge, holding water in reserve ready for use by plants. Clay soils with tiny particles and tiny air spaces hold the greatest amount of water. Sandy soils have larger pores, and although they fill up easily with water, this drains away quickly and is therefore not held in reserve for the plants. In general, you will have to water a sandy soil more often than a clay soil.

When it rains or when you water a soil, all the spaces become filled up with water and the soil becomes saturated. When the rain or irrigation stops, the excess water runs away, leaving the soil holding water within its pore spaces. This stage, where there is both air and plenty of water within the soil, is the ideal condition in which roots function and plants grow. As plants grow they remove the water from the soil until a stage is reached where they can remove no more and the plant starts to wilt.

If the excess moisture cannot drain away after rain or irrigation, the soil remains waterlogged. Under waterlogged conditions, roots do not thrive, as there is no air present, and may die if waterlogging persists. In this situation, with dead roots, the plant cannot take up water and so will wilt, which seems contradictory in a waterlogged situation.

Watering fruit and vegetables

Virtually all fruit and vegetables have a high water content so keeping crops irrigated in dry weather is highly desirable. In particular, greenhouses and containers will need regular watering. A tomato crop in the full flush of summer growth inside a greenhouse will have a massive daily requirement for water. Freshly transplanted crops or young fruit trees will need regular watering. Germinating seeds are also very sensitive but you must avoid damaging delicate seedlings or the soil structure. A heavy sprinkler pounding water on a seedbed is likely to cap the surface, preventing seedlings from emerging.

Individual crops will, however, have certain peak times in their growth sequence when water is most important. For example, raspberries must have adequate water when the fruits are swelling or they just shrivel. Tomatoes must have enough water when the flowers are ready for pollination or the fruit does not set, and potatoes must have generous supplies of water when the tubers are swelling.

In general, the principle should always be to apply liberal quantities of water to allow the soil to become fully charged, repeating this only when the soil is showing signs of drying. Frequent small applications of water are not recommended as they only dampen the surface and do not penetrate to the roots. Apply water thoroughly using a hose to get soils completely moist down to root levels. A good sprinkler with coarse droplets is preferable to a fine mist that will blow away or evaporate. It is best to irrigate in the evening or at night rather than in bright sunshine or windy conditions, when a proportion of the water will be lost by evaporation. A sunken flower pot next to a young tree helps to direct the water straight to the roots.

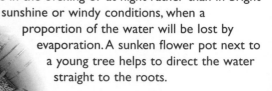

Water conservation

In this era of water shortages, we should emphasize the environmental importance of reducing the use of town water by storing rainwater. Various techniques and pieces of equipment are available to divert rainwater into a storage butt. It should be emphasized that such stored water is stagnant and may contain plant diseases, so should not be used in greenhouses or with any young seedlings.

It is also possible to use gray water, which is recycled water from your washing machine, bath and dishwasher. You can buy diverter kits which will channel this water into water butts or storage tanks. It is generally thought that it is safe to use such recycled water on most crops.

Mulching refers to the spreading of a "blanket" of material over the soil to help retain moisture by reducing evaporation. It also reduces weed growth. This is often a bulky organic material such as mushroom compost, shredded bark, or leaf mold. In the kitchen garden, straw, polythene, or a purpose-made horticultural fabric might be used.

Mulches should always be applied when the soil is already moist so that the water within the soil is trapped. Organic mulches will slowly break down and act as general soil improvers. They can also be important sources of nutrients, particularly trace elements. For example, soft fruit bushes or fruit trees can be annually mulched with farmyard manure. A mulch should be applied between 7.5–10 cm. (3–4 in.) deep to be effective. All mulches also help to regulate soil temperatures, keeping them cool in summer and warm in winter.

Feeding fruit and vegetables

All plants need nutrients to grow and develop, most of which come from the soil. The three main elements needed by plants are nitrogen, phosphorous, and potassium (sometimes called potash), collectively referred to as NPK, taking the letters from their chemical symbols. These are required in large quantities for growth. Generally one thinks of nitrogen as the nutrient that promotes leaf growth, phosphorous for roots, and potassium for flowers or fruit.

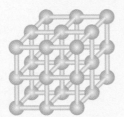

In addition, plants require a range of other elements in differing levels. Magnesium (Mg), calcium (Ca), and sulphur (S) are the next most important. Then there are those required in minute quantities, usually called trace elements. These include iron (Fe), manganese (Mn), copper (Cu), zinc (Zn), boron (Bo), molybdenum (Mb), and chlorine (Cl).

What's on the Packet?

By law all fertilizers have to be packaged with the analysis of contents on the outside. Each fertilizer will usually have a three-figure code, maybe 15–30–15, which refers to the proportions of NPK. Each may also have a detailed analysis of the percentage of each nutrient. This is useful to determine if trace elements are present. The packet should also have a rate of application or, in the case of liquid fertilizers, dilution. You should always read the instructions and never exceed the application rates recommended. In fact, applying a half-rate application then repeating at a later stage can be useful if there is any concern about causing scorch.

Nowadays there is a bewildering range of fertilizers available for use and products will be described in many different ways. Chemical or inorganic fertilizers are factory produced, generally cheap, and the type of fertilizers widely used in agriculture, for vegetable and fruit production or for fertilising lawns. Organic fertilizers originate from some sort of natural product and include fertilizers such as bonemeal or dried blood. They will generally be more expensive and slower in reaction than chemical fertilizers, as the material has to break down in the soil to release the nutrients.

Some Organic Fertilizers

✳ Dried blood—a good, fast acting source of nitrogen
✳ Hoof and horn—a slow-acting source of nitrogen
✳ Fish, blood, and bone – a mixture with nitrogen, phosphorus, and potassium
✳ Bonemeal—a good, slow-release source of phosphorous, ideal for planting fruit trees
✳ Chicken manure—often pelleted and a good source of nitrogen
✳ Seaweed meal—rich in trace elements

Compound or balanced fertilizers have a blend of different nutrients within them, supplying all of the plant's needs in one go. One of the most common would be Growmore, a cheap chemical fertilizer, widely used for vegetable production. Straight fertilizers are simple chemicals providing only one or two nutrients, for example superphosphate, sulfate, or potassium.

Slow-release fertilizers are generally the "Rolls Royces" of fertilizers, and will have all the nutrients required bound up in a small pill, which breaks down slowly within the soil, feeding the plants over a predictable span of time. Such fertilizers are very useful in providing a whole season's nutrients in one application.

Liquid feeds are fertilizers in a soluble form that have the advantage of giving a rapid response. They may be sold as a concentrated liquid that is diluted or as a soluble powder. In both cases they must be mixed with the correct amount of water before using. Liquid feeds should never be applied to a plant that is dry, as root scorch may occur. Some suppliers of liquid feeds produce their own diluters, which connect to a hose and make application an easy job.

Many of the above explanatory terms can be used together because they describe different aspects of a fertilizer. So, for example, we could have a slow-release, inorganic fertilizer, like many modern commercial products, or an organic ,balanced fertilizer such as blood, fish, and bone—a very smelly mixture of traditional constituents.

Using Fertilizers

A good base fertilizer for vegetable growing is Growmore, which can be used at a rate of 60 g./m.^{2} (2 oz./square yard) prior to sowing or planting almost any vegetables. A good organic alternative would be fish, blood, and bonemeal. When planting fruit trees or bushes during the winter months, a fertilizer with a high phosphate content, such as bonemeal, should be used to encourage root growth. Growmore can be used as a top dressing during the summer months to encourage balanced growth. This should be sprinkled along the rows, hoed in lightly, and then watered in. Crops such as tomatoes, zucchinis, or runner beans, that you will want to go on producing over an extended period of time, respond well to regular liquid feeding. In general, do not feed in the autumn, as any overwintering vegetables do not want soft lush growth that would be damaged by the winter cold.

Warning
Whenever handling fertilizers, it is wise to wear rubber gloves. Fertilizers can cause dermatitis or make the skin very dry. When applying large quantities, it is wise to wear a dust mask to avoid inhaling the finer particles.

Nutritional Deficiencies

Either a lack or an excess of certain nutrients will cause plants to suffer and show altered characteristics. Liquid or foliar feeds are the quickest ways to correct deficiencies. A lack of nitrogen will show as yellowing leaves and slow, stunted growth. Yellowing can also indicate a phosphorus deficiency, but this is very rare as most soils have sufficient quantities of phosphorus. Potassium deficiency will show as blue, yellow, or purple tints, especially at the edges of the leaves, which turn brown and die.

A deficiency of iron is very common in alkaline soils and shows as yellowing between the leaf veins (interveinal chlorosis). It is corrected with sequestered iron, which is readily available in garden centers. Magnesium deficiency often occurs with tomatoes, also showing as interveinal chlorosis and can be corrected with a liquid feed of Epsom salts dissolved in water, 20 g./lt. (2.5 oz./gall.). Shortages of other minerals and particularly trace elements are less common. Some can give odd symptoms such as a shortage of molybdenum on brassicas, causing a condition known as whiptail, which shows as narrow, deformed leaves which are not much more than a rib.

As trace elements are only needed in minute quantities, supplying them can be tricky. Soils which are regularly fed with organic matter are less likely to show trace element problems. In mid season, the simplest action is to use a liquid organic fertilizer, such as liquid seaweed, which contains all the trace elements.

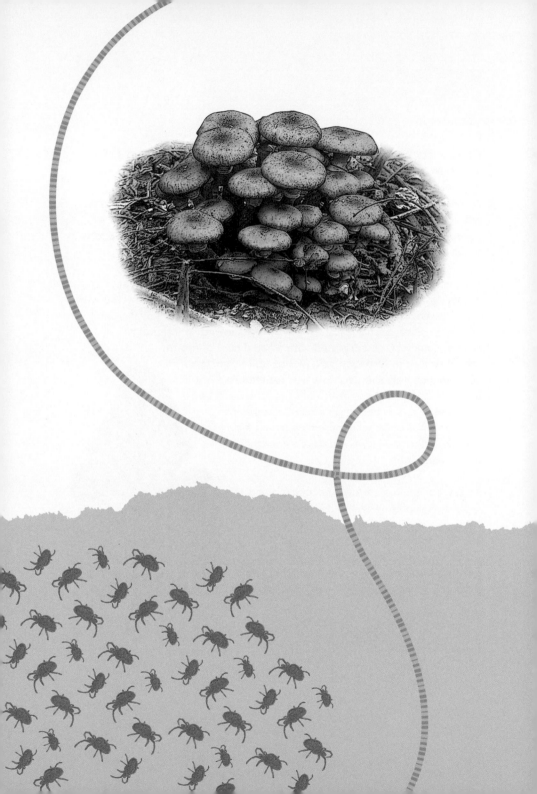

Pests and diseases

Sadly, many crops suffer from pests and diseases. A book such as this can only attempt to deal with a portion of those that may occur, but often these are variations on a basic problem. For example, there are many different types of aphid, greenfly, and blackfly that attack different crops. Crop-specific pests and diseases will be mentioned with the entry for each plant later in this book.

Control of pests and diseases

The control of pests and diseases has become far more difficult for the amateur gardener in recent years, as the range of pesticides available for dealing with plant pests is severely restricted. This, of course, is a good thing for both safety and environmental reasons and indeed many gardeners may wish to choose alternative, non-chemical treatments for pests and diseases.

Dealing with pests and diseases

The traditional method of controlling any pest or disease is to spray a chemical pesticide onto the plants to kill the pest. The side effects are possible contamination of the crop and the environment, and also potential destruction of beneficial creatures, such as ladybugs. The use of pesticides on fruit and vegetables always raises the question of residues left at harvest.

Beneficial Creatures

Many of the insects and other creatures that live on plants and in your garden are not pests but are beneficial in the garden. Be sure to differentiate between the friends and foes. Ladybugs, lacewings, spiders, and centipedes are all garden friends, which act as natural predators, feeding on pests. The ladybug is probably the most common example and eats many aphids each day to stay alive. Bees are, of course, pollinating insects and essential for many fruit crops. Larger creatures such as frogs, toads and hedgehogs are valuable, too, in controlling slugs. By minimizing the number of pesticides we use, we can encourage these beneficial creatures and move towards a situation where pests are held in check by natural means.

You should try to use a minimum of pesticides and, wherever possible, look for alternative ways of controlling pests. The effects of pests and diseases can be reduced by growing and feeding plants well, to make them healthy and able to withstand those pests and diseases. A weak, poorly fed plant is much more likely to succumb to attack. There are also varieties of fruit and vegetables that are resistant to diseases and sometimes pests. These are well worth growing. Certain techniques, such as crop rotation and companion planting, are also effective and are described with the relevant crops throughout this book.

Biological Control

The use of other creatures, which act as parasites or predators, is becoming well established and this is known as biological control. These creatures are available mail order from specialist firms. Many biological controls are specific and target just one pest but a new mix of nematodes is available, which controls a whole range of pests: carrot root fly, cabbage root fly, leatherjackets, cutworms, onion fly, sciarid, caterpillars, gooseberry sawfly, thrips, and codling moths are all controlled. Depending on the pest, the product is applied to the soil or the crop. These products are completely safe for use on edible crops and provide no risk to children, pets, or wildlife.

Companion planting

This is a technique of pest control whereby you plant different crops together. Generally the scent of one plant will mask another and so deter the pest. It is largely unproven but many gardeners practice it to some extent and report consistent levels of success. Growing spring onions amongst carrots will discourage carrot root fly. Nasturtiums can be used to mask the smell of brassicas and deter cabbage white butterflies. *Tagetes* planted in a greenhouse will dissuade whitefly from attacking tomatoes. Garlic is also said to deter many pests. Alternatively, a plant can be used that will attract a predator, which will naturally control the pest. French marigolds attract beneficial hoverflies, which feed on aphids so these are useful next to crops such as beans, which are liable to be attacked by aphids. Books on organic gardening will suggest many other "buddy plantings!"

Pesticides

When all else fails, you may still have to use a chemical pesticide but you should always aim to use the least toxic chemical for the job and use it in a safe way. This book can only give limited advice, as the availability of pesticides to amateurs is constantly changing. Most of the chemicals available on garden center shelves nowadays have relatively low toxicity and, if used in accordance with the recommendations and precautions, can be used quite safely. Many products, such as pyrethrum and derris, or simple materials such as soft soap, are based on naturally available ingredients.

Pesticides are described as contact or residual. Contact pesticides have an instant knock-down effect. Residual pesticides are taken in by the plant and kill the pest as it feeds on the plant. These are best for any pest, like leaf miner, that lives inside the plant. Contact pesticides are the safest for any food crops, as poisonous residues are not retained for so long. All pesticides will list a safe period that must be maintained between spraying and harvesting a crop for eating.

Safety measures when spraying

* Always wear protective clothing: gloves, goggles, and a dust mask.
* Keep children and pets away while spraying
* Never eat, drink, or smoke while spraying.
* Always follow the instructions.
* Do not spray in windy or very hot conditions in case of scorch.
* Early morning or evening is best to avoid harming bees.
* Dispose of excess chemical by spraying out on bare soil.
* Wash out sprayer after use.
* Never use the same sprayer for weed killers as pesticides.
* Wash clothes after spraying.
* Wash or shower yourself thoroughly after spraying.
* Make sure all chemicals are stored securely, away from children.
* With edible crops, always observe the safe period between spraying and harvesting.

The pests themselves

Pests are small creatures that live in or on plants, eating them for food. Some may be very obvious, such as slugs and snails. Other pests include greenfly and, smaller still, there are microscopic pests, such as eelworm, which live within the plants but still have devastating effects. Some pests carry other diseases; for example, greenfly on their own are a relatively harmless pest, but the viruses they spread can be extremely serious.

Slugs and snails

Probably the most hated of all pests, because of the devastating damage they do, slugs and snails are most active in wet weather and feed at night.

CONTROL—Blue slug pellets contain metaldehyde, which is highly toxic to children and pets. A newer product based on iron and phosphates breaks down to basic soil nutrients. Scatter pellets sparingly. Alternatively, spread sharp sand or crushed egg shells around plants, set up beer traps to drown slugs, or collect them at night by torchlight. Biological control in the form of nematode worms can be used.

Aphids

These include greenfly, blackfly, and also woolly aphids. Aphids are small, often winged, insects up to about 5 mm. (¼ in.) usually found on the undersides of leaves and around young growths. They suck the sap out of a plant, which weakens it and can turn the leaves yellow, leave a sticky excrement, which turns black and is called sooty mold, and spread viruses.

CONTROL—Contact insecticides, such as soft soap products, will have an immediate effect. Winter washes can be used to control the eggs of over-wintering aphids on fruit trees. Various biological controls are available.

Red spider mite

This is a pest that is often not noticed until there is a massive infestation. Red spider mites can affect garden plants such as fruit trees but they are more commonly seen on greenhouse plants, such as cucumbers, melons, or peppers. These are tiny creatures and so visible only as a fine, dust-like coating underneath leaves. For this reason they are often missed until the attack is well established, and the leaves show a dull yellow mottling, become brown, brittle, and drop. With a bad attack a fine mesh like a spider's web is formed around plant tips.

CONTROL—Under glass, the pest can be deterred by maintaining a damp atmosphere but this will not control an established infestation. Most readily available pesticides will not control red spider mite and a specific acaricide must be obtained. Alternatively, biological control by means of the predator *Phytoseilus* is very successful.

Whitefly

Commonly found on glasshouse plants, such as tomatoes and cucumbers, but also outside on crops, such as brassicas. The creature itself is like a tiny white moth, which flies off in large numbers when disturbed. They feed by sucking the sap from plants, living on the undersides of the leaf. They also leave behind sticky honeydew and sooty mold. They breed rapidly so numbers and damage can escalate fast.

CONTROL—Contact insecticides, such as soft soap, are reasonably effective, as are some of the synthetic pyrethroids. The trick with whitefly is to spray frequently at about four-day intervals, rotating the chemical used. Under glass, the parasite *Encarsia* is very effective, particularly on individual crops, such as tomatoes or cucumbers. It may have to be reintroduced several times in a season.

Flea beetles

Tiny jumping creatures that eat holes in crops, particularly in seedlings of members of the Brassica family, including radishes and turnips.

CONTROL—one of the easiest control measures is to drag a yellow sticky trap through the rows. The flea beetles jump and get trapped.

Leaf miner

A pest that lives inside the leaf and creates a distinct pattern, leaving twisting, whitish tunnels as it moves through the leaf, feeding. With a bad attack, the tunnels will end up linked together into large, blister-like patches which turn yellow and brown. In the vegetable garden they can be found on celery, tomatoes, and mint.

CONTROL—This is difficult, as the pest is inside the leaf and many pesticides will not control it. When there is relatively little damage, either destroy the individual creatures with your thumbnail or pick off infected leaves. Removing too many leaves, however, will slow down the plant's growth.

Vine weevil

This pest can be found on a wide range of plants and can sometimes be brought in with new plants from a garden center. The adult vine weevil is an ugly grayish beetle that eats notches out of leaves. It disfigures plants but rarely causes major damage. The larva, which is the juvenile stage, is a small white grub, up to 1 cm. (½ in.) long with a brown head. This causes major damage, as it lives on the roots of plants, which wilt and eventually die. Outside it particularly attacks strawberries, raspberries, and blackcurrants.

CONTROL—If vine weevil is suspected in potted plants, the simplest treatment is to tip it out and examine the roots. If infected, wash the roots thoroughly, removing the infected compost and grubs. Repot in fresh compost and keep in a damp atmosphere until re-established. Surprisingly, plants will often recover from such drastic treatment. With a more widespread problem outdoors, it is possible to use a chemical root drench of Armillatox. Biological controls are not so effective against this pest outdoors.

Caterpillars

These come in a whole host of sizes and colors, often camouflaged to hide in the plants they are feeding on. Cabbage white caterpillars are common on Brassica crops. Tortrix and winter moth are pests of fruit trees. Damage occurs in the summer. Many others may be a problem.

CONTROL—On a small scale, hand-picking is both effective and very safe. Contact insecticides can be used. A biological control based on the bacteria *Bacillus* is also available for use on Brassicas. Winter washes are valuable in controlling the overwintering eggs on fruit trees. Winter moth caterpillars can be controlled with grease bands applied to the trunk in mid autumn. These trap the wingless female moth as she climbs from the ground into the tree to lay eggs, which will ultimately become caterpillars.

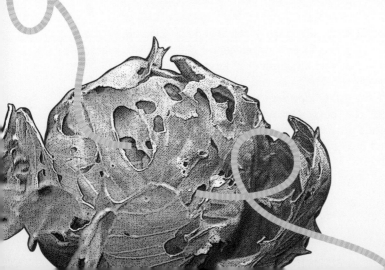

Diseases

These are distinct from pests in that they are caused by another organism such as a fungus, bacteria, or virus. Diseases may attack any part of the plant, including the root system. Sometimes the effects may be clearly visible as a mold on the leaf surface, or a distortion, whereas other diseases may be inside the plant and only show as the plant's health declines.

The control of diseases is slightly different to the control of pests, in that many diseases such as mildew or botrytis are very difficult to eradicate once they are established on a plant. The emphasis is therefore on prevention. Initially it is good practice to modify conditions where plants are growing to deter diseases. However with some plants and situations where diseases are particularly likely to occur, some gardeners will choose to use a preventative spray of a fungicide to protect the plant. For example, this is often done with seedlings in a greenhouse to protect them from damping off disease. The spray or drench will need to be repeated at intervals to maintain the protection.

Powdery mildew

Many plants suffer from this, particularly apples and peas. It is immediately visible as a white mealy deposit over leaves and sometimes flowers or fruit. Strangely while it is most prevalent on plants in dry conditions, it spreads from plant to plant in damp weather and by means of water splashes. So a rainy spell followed by dry weather is an ideal set of conditions for a mildew outbreak.

CONTROL—Do not let susceptible plants go short of water. With important crops, use a protective fungicide spray as a routine precaution. Vary the fungicides to avoid resistance developing.

Rusts

There are many different types of rust affecting different plants. Rust usually appears as bright orange or brown patches on the undersides of leaves, with a yellow spot showing on the upper surface. Rusts are not particularly common on vegetables, but may appear on asparagus, tomatoes, and beans. A particular type of rust may infect apples.

CONTROL—Affected leaves can be removed and burnt or a protective fungicide spray used if susceptible plants are being grown.

Botrytis (gray mold)

This fungal infection can attack almost any plant, although soft, young plants are most likely to succumb. It is also most prevalent under poor conditions, such as a cool greenhouse early in the year, when the light is poor and growth is weak. It shows as a gray, fuzzy mold on leaves, shoots or in the growing points of plants. The tissues underneath this rapidly go mushy and rot.

CONTROL—Avoidance is, as always, best, which in this instance means trying to grow strong, healthy plants. In greenhouses, good ventilation and air circulation helps. There are a number of commercial fungicides available to combat botrytis, several tailored to specific plants. Preventative sprays used in advance of an attack are also effective. These are sometimes used on susceptible seedlings and crops, such as glasshouse lettuce, in winter.

Armillaria

Also known as honey fungus, because of the honey-colored toadstools that are eventually produced. This devastating disease attacks fruit trees and woody plants, such as soft fruit bushes. Initially it will show as a general yellowness of leaves, followed by wilting. Quite quickly the plant will start to die and large trees can go from appearing healthy to being dead within a single season.

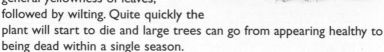

The presence of this disease can be confirmed in two ways. Scrape the bark near ground level and check for the presence of a white mold that smells of mushrooms. Alternatively dig down to the root system and look to see if there are any black, thread-like growths. These give the disease the alternative name "boot-lace fungus." It easily spreads from plant to plant through the soil. For example, on hedges, which are particularly susceptible, you can see the disease working its way down the row.

CONTROL—Initially, infected plants should be dug up and burnt. You can use a soil drench of Armillatox to prevent further spread, especially if there are other valuable trees or bushes nearby. Soil infected with armillaria can only be used for non-woody plants—vegetables are not susceptible. Replacement of the soil is possible but large quantities will usually have to be dug out and it is difficult to be sure that all the fungus has been removed.

Viruses

A wide variety of plants are attacked by virus diseases, although they are less likely on annual plants, such as fast-growing vegetables, as viruses are less commonly seed transmitted. Both tomatoes and cucumbers, however, can suffer from viruses. They cause a wide variety of symptoms, which include distortion of leaves or flowers, spotting, mosaic patterns or streaking and reduction in vigor or cropping potential. Viruses rarely kill plants completely but they can so distort or weaken a plant that it is no longer productive. Viruses in fruit plantations, such as the reversion virus of blackcurrants, are more serious because the only real treatment is to destroy the crop and start again.

CONTROL—Viruses are almost impossible to control. In general garden terms, if a plant has acquired a virus, it is infected for life. This is not entirely true as there are sophisticated techniques by which specialist nurseries can produce virus-free stock under laboratory conditions. So for example, you may see virus-free stock of old favorites such as the "Royal Sovereign" strawberry offered for sale.

In general, virus-infected plants should be dug up and destroyed. Viruses are usually spread by sap-sucking insects such as aphids, so these should be controlled to avoid the spread of the virus. Viruses can also be passed from plant to plant on a propagating knife. So where plants are propagated by cuttings, the knife or pruning shears should ideally be sterilized between cuts, by passing through a flame or with a horticultural disinfectant. One pest that produces similar

symptoms to virus is eelworm.
These are tiny microscopic
worms that live inside the
leaves and cause distortion.
They may appear on onions,
peas, beans, cucumber,
tomato, salad crops, and
soft fruits—most
especially strawberries.
They are a particular
problem for potatoes,
where the swollen bodies of
the egg-laden females can be
seen as cysts on the roots. Things
are never simple!

Cultural problems

Just to complicate issues, there are a host of other problems that can
adversely affect plants and that cannot be blamed on pests or diseases. When
the situations in which plants grow are less than ideal, plants will start to
suffer and show various symptoms. Gardeners always blame
the weather! And indeed plants are very sensitive to
changes in conditions or excesses. High temperatures
will cause scorch, as will frost, high winds, or shortage
of water. Excess water causes roots to die, resulting in
wilting. Low light will cause plants to be thin, spindly,
and pale. Plants growing in greenhouses are particularly
likely to suffer from these excesses. When plants are
affected by wrong feeding, they will also show nutritional
deficiencies or excesses (this is dealt with on page 35).

Growing vegetables

Most vegetables are fast-growing crops that will progress from the seed packet to harvest in a matter of weeks. Such crops are rewarding for all gardeners, but particularly so for new growers and children. Most are easy to grow and very forgiving if you don't treat them quite right! And, for adults and children alike, there's nothing quite like eating the vegetables you have grown.

Buying seeds

Most vegetable crops are raised annually from seeds and a good catalog will show an amazing range of varieties. Do not be tempted to buy the cheapest seeds. Many of the best varieties are F1 hybrids and, because of their special breeding, will be more expensive. They are nevertheless worth the extra premium because of their added characteristics, such as vigor, heavier cropping, and disease resistance.

As well as natural seed, some vegetable seeds may be available in special forms. Some seeds may come pre-treated with a fungicide to protect against diseases. Other tiny seeds such as lettuce are available as pellets, which consist of a seed with a coating that makes them bigger and easier to handle. One enterprising seed merchant is now offering small seeded species that have been coated and colored for easy handling.

All seed should last a full twelve months but many will last several years if stored carefully. Generally, the larger seeds, such as peas and beans store the longest, while smaller seeds, such as papery parsnips and carrots have a shorter storage span. If you have used part of a packet, seal the packet again and store in a cool, dry place. This is useful for crops where you may want just a few plants or a short row each year. Seeds such as peas and beans which have been stored for a couple of years can be helped in their germination by soaking them in warm water for twenty-four hours before sowing.

Award of Garden Merit

Plants designated as AGM have been awarded this standard by the Royal Horticultural Society, often following competitive trials at one of their gardens. Such plants, available throughout the world, must have outstanding performance, be easy to grow, resistant to pests and diseases and be readily available. Wherever possible these varieties have been recommended in this book.

In general, do not be tempted to save your own seed. Vegetables do not necessarily breed true and seed saved from a very successful crop may be mediocre the next year. This is particularly so with F1 hybrids, which never breed true.

Crop rotations and planning

Using a crop rotation is a very traditional way of managing a vegetable plot or allotment. Basically, similar vegetable types are grouped together in order to give them the conditions they like for growth and to avoid a build-up of pests and diseases. The three main groups are brassicas, including cabbages, cauliflowers, and Brussels sprouts; secondly root crops, including carrots, parsnips, beetroot, and potatoes; and thirdly legumes, the whole range of peas and beans. You can make a fourth group with miscellaneous and tender vegetables such as zucchinis, sweetcorn, celery, and tomatoes.

The plot is then divided into three or four areas and the crop groups moved around over a three- or four-year period. In this way we can hope to avoid the build-up of pests and diseases that can occur when crops are always grown on the same land. You should also try to treat the soil in the ideal way for each crop. Peas and beans are rich feeders so try to add manure or organic matter before these crops. Brassicas need a high pH so aim to lime before these crops. Root crops do not like lumpy organic matter in the soil, as the roots will be misshapen, so aim to grow these one or two years after manuring, so the manure will be well absorbed into the soil. Salads are not particularly fussy and can be squeezed in wherever there is a gap. Onions can be put with root vegetables.

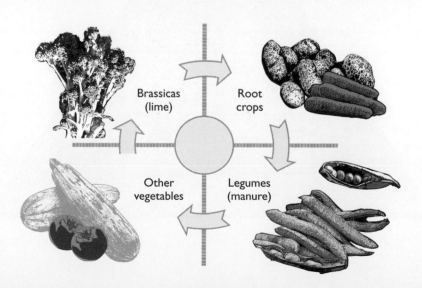

Brassicas
(lime)

Root
crops

Other
vegetables

Legumes
(manure)

Bed systems

This is simply the technique of growing vegetables in beds that are narrow enough to tend from the pathways either side. Naturally bed systems fit well into the small garden situation rather than an extensive allotment. Raised beds are particularly useful when gardening on a clay soil. As you improve a clay soil with grit and compost it will bulk up and the raised growing medium will more easily drain. Also, being able to stretch across the bed means you don't need to tread on and further compact a sticky soil. Raised beds can easily be covered with fleece if frost is forecast.

There are various expensive raised bed kits on the market but these are not essential. Unless they are very deep, most raised soil areas will retain their shape. If you want to enclose them for tidiness, try using recycled timber, such as old scaffold boards or scrap decking. Where there is soil underneath, a depth of 15–30 cm. (6–12 in.) is adequate but if you are constructing raised beds over concrete, 30 cm. (12 in.) would be the minimum, ideally more. With raised beds, you can still carry out crop rotation, allocating smaller units to the various groups of crops.

Succession and intercropping

Continuity is all important and you should aim to produce crops that you can continue to harvest over many weeks, maybe the whole summer. The classic mistake is to grow too much of one thing. With many crops this will mean making a number of sowings at different stages so that the crops mature at different intervals. With some crops you will also need to use early, mid- and late-season varieties that mature at different times.

Succession also involves the continued use of the space in a vegetable garden. So for example, when a crop of spring cabbage has been harvested in late spring, the ground can be cleared and cultivated ready to take a row of celery that will mature later in the summer.

Intercropping is quite simply making the best of limited space by juggling one crop between another. So for example, sweetcorn, which is slow growing and will not be mature until the end of summer, would be planted at least 45 cm. (18 in.) apart. It is quite possible to grow a crop of lettuce between the sweetcorn, which is finished by mid--summer. Sometimes this will mean planting or sowing the quick crop first, leaving space for the later main crop, which is planted in between. Avoid planting crops too closely together, which would risk spoiling one of the crops.

Soil preparation and seed sowing

Prepare the soil for growing vegetables by digging in advance, ideally over winter. In the spring as the soil starts to dry, finish the seedbed by breaking down the surface into a fine crumbly tilth, using a fork and rake. If the soil is not sticky, you can tread the soil at this stage, which breaks the clods and gently firms the surface. Apply a general balanced fertilizer, such as Growmore, at 60 g./m.^{2} (2 oz./square yards) or an organic alternative, before a final raking. Remove excess stones, remaining clods and any weeds. The surface should be fine and crumbly but not dusty. Such preparation is basic to virtually all vegetable crops in this guide. Ideally, prepare your seedbed well in advance of sowing and leave empty to allow the first crop of weeds to germinate so you can then hoe them off before seed sowing.

Most seeds are sown in a drill, which is a narrow v-shaped shallow channel. Traditionally, this is made with a draw hoe running alongside a tightly stretched garden line. You may find it easier to use a straight edge, such as a plank, and to scratch out a drill using a stick or bamboo cane. The depth of the drill is very important, as seeds should be sown at a depth of no more than twice their diameter, which is very shallow for small seeds, often less than 1 cm. (½ in.).

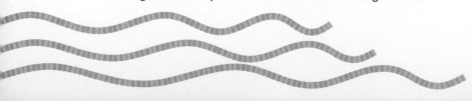

Sow seeds very thinly, bearing in mind the eventual spacing required. For example, lettuces will be thinned to about 30 cm. (12 in.) and parsnips to about 15 cm. (6 in.). If the seeds are large enough, you can individually sow at the final spacing, allowing a couple of seeds at each station. If both grow, remove one seedling later. After sowing, the soil is gently raked back into the drill to cover the seed. If conditions are dry, you can run water along the drill before sowing but it is not good to water after sowing as this can pan the soil down and inhibit germination.

Vegetable crops

Brassicas

This large group of vegetables includes cabbages, Brussels sprouts, and curly kale, all grown for their edible leaves, cauliflower, and broccoli for their flower heads, and rutabagas, and turnips for their roots.

Early summer brassicas

These are a range of fast-growing cabbages, cauliflowers, and broccoli that produce a welcome, early-summer crop.

SOWING—These should be sown under glass in early spring. Sow the seeds in modules to give small plants to plant out in mid- spring. Cauliflowers in particular must not suffer a check to growth so it is best to raise plants in 9 cm. (3½ in.) pots

CULTIVATION—Cabbages are spaced at about 45 cm. (18 in.) apart and cauliflowers at 60 cm. (2 ft.). Bend or break the leaves over cauliflower heads to prevent sun damaging them as the heads mature. Broccoli, sometimes called calabrese, can be grown in the same way. Space broccoli much closer, at about 30 cm. (12 in.) apart both ways.

HARVESTING—Harvest cauliflowers when the head is fully expanded in early summer. Broccoli will produce a central head and several pickings of smaller spears.

RECOMMENDED SUMMER BRASSICAS
Cabbage "Hispi" AGM—*fast-maturing, early-summer, pointed cabbage*
Cauliflower "Mayflower" AGM—*vigorous, early, very white*
Broccoli "Green Magic" AGM—*early variety with large heads*

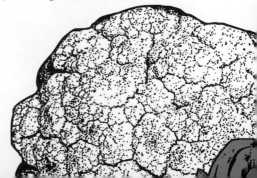

Winter Brassicas

These include Brussels sprouts, savoy cabbages, and winter cauliflower, which are all slow-growing but provide valuable green vegetables in winter months. They are tough and hardy and the flavor is often best when the crops have had a touch of frost.

SOWING—Sow in late spring, in modules, or in a seedbed outside, lifting and transplanting the seedlings when they have three or four leaves.

CULTIVATION—Plant them about 60 cm. (12 in.) apart. Plant winter brassicas slightly deeper than normal, to give good anchorage. Keep free of weeds, water in dry spells and feed once a month with a topdressing of a balanced fertilizer hoed into the surface.

HARVESTING—This can take place from early winter onwards according to varieties. Most will hold well in low winter temperatures and so storage is not really an issue. Small Brussels sprouts can, however, be frozen.

RECOMMENDED WINTER BRASSICAS
Cabbage "Celtic" AGM—*a round, Dutch white type, hardy and reliable*
Cabbage "Ruby Ball" AGM—*solid dark red heads for pickling or cooking*
Brussels sprouts "Nelson" AGM—*early cropping, sweet flavor, easy to harvest*
Cauliflower "Aalsmeer" AGM—*very winter hardy*

Spring cabbage and sprouting broccoli

Spring cabbages have hearts like any other cabbage, but spring greens just produce loose leaves. Sprouting broccoli produces a crop of broccoli spears in either white or purple in late spring.

SOWING—Sprouting broccoli is sown in late spring in a seedbed and transplanted to its final location when seedlings have about four leaves. Spring cabbage is sown in late summer and transplanted before winter.

CULTIVATION—Plant them about 60 cm. (12 in.) apart. Broccoli plants are tall and may require staking. All should be given an early spring feed of a nitrogenous fertilizer.

HARVESTING—Crops will be ready in late spring. Sprouting broccoli will yield several pickings continuing into early summer.

RECOMMENDED SPRING BRASSICAS
Cabbage "April"—*compact, pointed heads, hardy*
Broccoli "White Sprouting"—*similar but white in color and small spears*
Broccoli "Claret" AGM—*modern F1 hybrid, high-yield purple spears*

Pests and Diseases in brassicas
Brassicas suffer from cabbage white caterpillars, whitefly, mealy cabbage aphids, and cabbage root fly. The latter can be deterred from laying its eggs on a young plant by putting a small collar around the plant. Caterpillars can be hand-picked, and there is also a biological agent available. Brassicas are often attacked by pigeons. Netting the crop can protect them. Seedlings also suffer from flea beetle damage.

A fungal disease called club root can be devastating. It survives in old vegetable gardens for many years. It can be deterred by ensuring a high soil pH and by raising strong healthy plants in containers, which get a good head start. Some modern varieties have inbred resistance.

Legumes

This is the family of podded vegetables that we more generally refer to as peas and beans. Sometimes we eat the whole pod, as in runner beans or sugar peas, and with others, such as broad beans or peas, we eat the seed itself and dispose of the pod.

Members of this family of plants are said to be "nitrogen-fixing," as they have the ability to take nitrogen from the air and use it for growth. Despite this, all legumes are heavy feeders and so benefit from a general dressing of a balanced fertilizer before sowing or planting. When clearing pea and bean crops at the end of the season, it is useful to dig in the roots, as the remaining fixed nitrogen will stay in the soil for the next crop.

Runner beans
These are a valuable summer crop, particularly because they will go on producing for many weeks. Some runner beans are referred to as stringless and will require less preparation in the kitchen.

SOWING—Runner beans are tender plants and will not withstand frost so they should not be sown outside until late spring. The large seeds can be individually sown, putting two seeds at each planting station, usually 15–20 cm. (6–9 in.) apart. Plant with a dibber or small trowel, placing them about 2.5 cm. (1 in.) deep. If both seeds grow, remove the weakest plant or transplant to fill any gaps. Alternatively, they can be sown in small pots under glass and planted out in early summer as soon as all danger of frost has passed.

CULTIVATION—They are climbing plants, so must be provided with a support of some sort. Bamboo canes, 2.4 m. (8 ft.) in length, can be used to make either wigwams or a crossed double row. Alternatively, if available, tall brushwood can be used to make a thick "hedge," up which the beans can climb. Plastic nets are also available but will need a substantial support of poles and wire.

As soon as the stems start to elongate, they should be tucked in and encouraged to climb. Once started, they will climb on their own. Runner beans are very sensitive to water. If they are dry when in flower, the young pods will fall off, so it is essential to keep them well watered. Feed them regularly with a liquid feed to stimulate continued flowering and cropping.

HARVESTING—Pick regularly when they start to crop in mid--summer. They will continue to produce, if well fed and watered, until mid--autumn. A glut of runner beans can be frozen for winter use.

RECOMMENDED RUNNER BEANS

"St George" AGM—*very heavy cropping and good flavor, semi-stringless*

"Enorma" AGM—*huge bean, good for exhibition*

"Painted Lady"—*delightful and pretty variety with red/white flowers, reasonable crop*

"Lady Di" AGM—*stringless type, heavy cropping and good flavor*

PESTS AND DISEASES—Runner beans tend to suffer from aphids and slugs. Halo blight may occur, which causes brown spots with yellow surrounds, and anthracnose will cause brown patches on the beans. Infected plants of both should be destroyed.

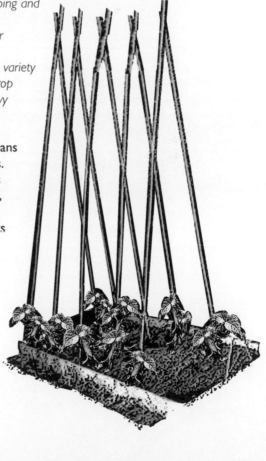

French beans

These are less commonly grown than runner beans but when harvested young make a wonderful tender and tasty vegetable. As well as green-podded varieties there are curious purple ones and particularly succulent yellow varieties.

SOWING—They are not hardy, so sowing should not start until mid--spring but can continue until early summer. They tend to have a shorter cropping life so it is worth making two or three sowings to give continuity. They should be sown in a single row, placing the seeds about 10 cm. (4 in.) apart and the rows about 45 cm. (18 in.) apart. These can also be sown slightly earlier under glass, using small pots and planting out in early summer.

CULTIVATION—A general balanced fertilizer, such as Growmore, applied at 60 g./m.^{2} (2 oz./square yards) before sowing should provide adequate nutrition for the crop. French beans generally have a bush habit, although there are a few climbing versions. Keep well watered during dry conditions.

HARVESTING—Cropping will usually be from mid--summer to mid-- autumn. Pick the beans while very young or they become stringy. Regular picking also stimulates continued cropping. French beans freeze well. The variety "borlotto" produces attractive red and cream marbled pods which can be left to mature and the beans dried for use in winter.

RECOMMENDED FRENCH BEANS
"Safari" AGM—*very slender and tender, 'filet' beans, fast growing, disease resistant*
"Purple Queen"—*purple pods, heavy yield, excellent flavor, green on cooking*
"Valdor"—*golden yellow color, great flavor, disease resistant*
"Borlotto"—*novelty with red mottled pods, can also mature and dry beans*
"'Cobra"—*a climbing French bean, grown like runner beans, long cropping season*

PESTS AND DISEASES—They suffer from slugs and aphids but are otherwise generally trouble-free.

Broad beans

These are a useful hardy crop, which will be ready for use in late spring.

SOWING—Sow mid-autumn or early spring. Broad beans are usually sown in a double row about 20 cm. (8 in.) apart, placing the seeds about 20 cm. (8 in.) apart. Multiple rows can be placed 60 cm. (2 ft.) from the next. The seeds are usually sown directly in the ground, about 5 cm. (2 in.) deep, although they too can be raised in small pots or modules and planted out.

CULTIVATION—They are generally self-supporting but it is a useful precaution to surround the double rows with a ring of string stretched between short posts. Water the crop if conditions are dry during flowering and pod formation. As soon as the first pods start to show, remove the tip of the plants as this concentrates the plant's energies into the crop. It also helps to discourage blackfly, which are attracted to the soft tips.

HARVESTING—An autumn sowing will usually give a useful late spring crop. Sowings made in spring will crop by early summer. Harvest as soon as the beans start to swell in the pods.

RECOMMENDED BROAD BEANS
"Aquadulce" AGM—*early crop, hardy and good for autumn sowing*
"The Sutton" AGM—*a dwarf type, ideal for small gardens, good cropper*
"Karmazyn"—*new and unusual variety with pink beans inside green pods.*

PESTS AND DISEASES—Blackfly is a serious pest of broad beans and can decimate the crop. It is worth spraying as soon as it appears to keep it under control.

Peas

Although frozen peas provide an easy way of sourcing a vegetable that is fiddly to grow, there is nothing quite like freshly picked green peas. Peas are nevertheless a demanding crop and require a great deal of space for a relatively small crop, but it is worth growing the real thing at least once.

As well as the familiar garden peas, there are also mange tout and sugar snap peas, which are eaten complete with the tender pods.

Mange touts are eaten when the pods are flat, whereas sugar snap types are eaten when the peas within the pod have started to flesh out. There are also petit pois types, which produce tiny, very sweet peas, which are shelled, cooked and eaten like normal peas.

Peas are generally hardy, although some are tougher than others. They are divided into round- (smooth) and wrinkled-seeded varieties. The round seeded varieties are the toughest and the earliest to crop. The wrinkled types are larger, sweeter, and heavier cropping, although less hardy so sown later. Peas are also divided into early and maincrop varieties. By using a range of varieties, you can produce crops of peas from late spring through until mid-autumn.

SOWING—Generally the first sowings take place in early spring, although in sheltered areas it is possible to make a late autumn sowing. Early sowings should use a round-seeded early variety, moving on through the categories to maincrop wrinkled-seeded types, which can be sown from late spring through to early or mid-summer. Peas are sown in a flat-bottomed drill about 15 cm. (6 in.) wide. Individual peas are scattered or spaced about 7.5 cm. (3 in.) apart. The spacing between the rows should be about the same as the expected height of the crop.

CULTIVATION—Peas are climbing plants, so they will need some support, which is usually best provided as short brushwood or netting stretched between wooden stakes. Place the supports as soon as the seedlings emerge. Keep the plants well watered in any dry spells, particularly as the pods are swelling. If they become too dry, the crop will not set or develop and powdery mildew is also likely to appear.

HARVESTING—Peas tend to have one main flush of pods but healthy well-grown plants will produce some extra pods for a short while.

RECOMMENDED FIRST EARLIES—sow mid-autumn or early spring
"Little Marvel" AGM—*dwarf, very early and hardy*
"Early Onward" AGM—*heavy cropper, easy grower*
RECOMMENDED MAINCROP—sow early spring to early summer
"Onward" AGM—*heavy crop, resistant to fusarium wilt, good for exhibition*
"Hurst Greenshaft" AGM—*superb taste, easy grower, resistant to mildew*
RECOMMENDED OTHER PEAS
"Oregon Sugar Pod" AGM—*Mange tout type, gather and cook young*
"Sugar Snap Delikett" AGM—*sugar snap type, sweet flavor*
"Calibra"—*very sweet and tender petit pois type, good disease resistance*

PESTS AND DISEASES—Freshly sown peas are very attractive to both birds and mice. Protect from birds with black cotton tightly stretched between short canes or with wire netting guards. Traps can be set for mice. The most likely pest is pea moth, which causes maggoty peas. This is prevented by spraying with a suitable pesticide seven to ten days after flowering. Powdery mildew may occur, particularly if the crop is allowed to become too dry. Silvery patches on pods may be caused by thrips. The pea and bean weevil chops notches out of the leaves. Older plants are not severely damaged but if it appears early at seedling stage, it can be devastating. Damping off and wilt problems can also sometimes occur. Rotation helps to avoid these.

Root vegetables

These are easily grouped together, simply because we eat the swollen roots of all of them and their culture is similar. Some are eaten while very young and tender, such as baby carrots, but many will also produce mature, hardy roots that will supply the kitchen throughout the winter.

Carrots

These well-known vegetables can be harvested almost throughout the year. Most carrots are long and slender, although there are shorter, stump-rooted types, such as "Parmex." In recent years, several well-flavored, novelty types have been developed that are yellow, white, wine red, or purple.

SOWING—They can be sown from early spring through to early summer to produce a crop from early summer through until the winter. Carrots must generally be sown directly in the ground where they are to mature, as they will not tolerate transplanting. Sow in shallow, 1 cm. (½ in.) drills about 15 cm. (6 in. apart). Sow the seed very thinly to reduce the need for thinning, which attracts the carrot root fly.

CULTIVATION—Carrots grow best in light, sandy but moisture-retentive soils. They appreciate organic matter but any lumps, or stones in the soil will cause the roots to fork and distort. They do not have a high fertilizer requirement but use a normal base dressing prior to sowing. If tiny, tender, young carrots are wanted, these can be harvested early without any thinning. For bigger carrots and those you wish to mature for winter use, thin to about 5–7.5 cm. (2–3 in.) apart and water in after thinning to minimise disturbance. Provide regular watering to keep the roots tender and succulent during dry weather.

HARVESTING—Young carrots can be harvested for immediate use throughout the summer. Mature carrots can be harvested prior to the winter and stored in a traditional clamp or the rows covered with straw.

RECOMMENDED CARROTS
"Amsterdam Forcing 3" AGM—*fast, early, baby carrots, top of the taste tests*
"Parmex" AGM—*early globe-rooted carrots, can be grown in containers*
"Autumn King 2" AGM—*maincrop, good size, stands and keeps well*
"Flyaway" AGM—*sweet and tasty maincrop, resistant to carrot root fly*
"Purple Haze"—*one of the novelties, purple skin, red core, great taste*
"Yellowstone"—*golden yellow flesh, high in vitamins and beta-carotene*

PESTS AND DISEASES—Carrot root fly is a serious problem and the crop can be rendered unusable. The adult carrot fly lays eggs at the base of the carrot plants. The resulting young maggots feed on the carrot roots. Young seedlings will be killed completely. Older plants will show a reddish discoloration of the foliage and the roots will be mined with tunnels and black rotting areas.

There are no chemicals currently available to control this pest but there are several alternative cultural controls. Techniques are based on the fact that the adult carrot root fly is attracted by the smell of carrots. Companion planting with alternate rows of onions helps to mask the effect, as can mixing spring onion seeds in with the carrot seed at sowing stage. Avoiding thinning or other disturbance to the crop also helps. Delaying the sowing of maincrop varieties until June helps, as this avoids the peak season of attack. Covering the rows with a horticultural fleece will protect them. Finally, surrounding the crop with clear plastic, at least 60 cm. (2 ft.) tall, seems to deter the fly, as the females are low flying. Some varieties are less susceptible to damage, although not totally resistant.

Parsnips

This strongly flavored root vegetable is quite easy to grow and either a firm favourite or equally detested. It is a valuable, hardy, winter crop.

SOWING—Parsnips like a long growing season so sow thinly in early spring, in rows 30 cm. (12 in. apart)

CULTIVATION—They have a low fertilizer requirement but use the normal base dressing in advance of sowing. Thin seedlings to 15 cm. (6 in.) apart. Other than keeping them weed free and well watered, they need little attention.

HARVESTING—Parsnips are ready in autumn but some would say that the best flavor develops after the crop has had a frost. They are totally hardy and can be dug through the winter

RECOMMENDED PARSNIPS
'Tender and True' AGM—*reliable variety, good flavor, good crop, canker resistant*
'Gladiator' AGM—*delicious flavor and canker resistant, also good for exhibition*

PESTS AND DISEASES—They are relatively free of pests and diseases, although can occasionally attract canker, carrot root fly or lettuce root aphids. To avoid canker, don't sow too early, keep well watered and choose resistant varieties.

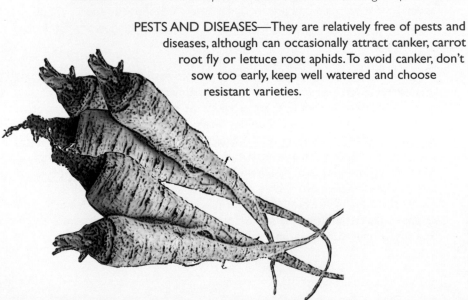

Rutabaga and turnips

Rutabagas are another traditional winter root vegetable and good for stews and roasting. They are grown very much as parsnips are but sow a little later for harvesting late autumn and winter. Turnips, a humble vegetable, are often much maligned. If harvested while young and cooked carefully, the flavor can be superb. If left to get old and mature, the flavor is stronger and they need then to be used for stews and similar dishes. As well as white roots, both golden- and pink-skinned types are available. Although both rutabaga and turnip are root vegetables, they are best grown with brassicas, as they suffer from the same pests and diseases.

SOWING—Sow thinly about 1 cm. (½ in.) deep, in rows 30 cm. (12 in.) apart from early spring through to early summer. Successional sowings may be made, although some varieties bolt in hot weather.

CULTIVATION—Thin to about 10 cm. (4 in.) and keep weed free and well watered.

HARVESTING—Ready from late spring through to autumn. Mature roots can be stored in a traditional clamp.

RECOMMENDED TURNIPS
"Golden Ball"—*hardy but best eaten young, tender yellow flesh*
"Atlantic" AGM—*very early, purple-topped roots, bolt-resistance*
"Tokyo Cross" AGM—*fast growing, pure white, high yields, good flavor*
RECOMMENDED RUTABAGAS
"Ruby" AGM—*sweet flesh, hardy and mildew resistant*
"Marian"—*purple skin, good flavor, clubroot and mildew resistant*

PESTS AND DISEASES—They are relatively free from pests and diseases, although seedlings may attract flea beetles and can be prone to clubroot.

Beetroot

Most people are familiar with the vividly colored, red root vegetable, often picked and served with salads. Fewer people know the easily grown and quite delicious golden beet. When baked and served with butter, it is a mouth-watering vegetable.

SOWING—Beetroot are slightly tender and so should not be sown until mid-spring through to early summer. Sow thinly about 2.5 cm. (1 in.) deep in rows about 30 cm. (12 in.) apart. Despite being a root crop, beetroot can be sown under cover in modules, providing they are planted out while young.

CULTIVATION—Thin seedlings to 10 cm. (4 in.) apart, water in dry weather and keep weed free.

HARVESTING—Ready for use as soon as about golf-ball size from mid-summer to early autumn. Use fresh or can be pickled in vinegar for winter use.

RECOMMENDED BEETROOTS

"Boltardy" AGM—*good for early sowing, bolt resistance, good flavor*
"Red Ace" AGM—*high quality, stands well, good to eat and for show*
"Burpees Golden"—*golden yellow roots with excellent flavor*

PESTS AND DISEASES—Beetroot tend to be generally free from common pests and diseases. Occasionally you may see mangold fly damage, which is a type of leaf miner. Black fly may be troublesome. Beetroot are also sensitive to trace element deficiencies, which may cause strange foliage symptoms.

Potatoes

This vegetable needs little introduction. Potatoes take up a great deal of space so are really only feasible if you have a large garden or allotment. However, young, freshly dug new potatoes have a flavor that is second to none and virtually always lost when bought in shops. For this reason it is worth trying to grow a few early potatoes if nothing else. And don't forget to grow some mint to go with them! Always buy good-quality seed potatoes as these will be virus free. Home-saved potatoes may be harbouring all sorts of pests and diseases and should not be used.

CHITTING AND PLANTING—The potato is a tuber and the plant that grows from it is tender, so you must not allow it to be subjected to frost. In early spring, set the seed potatoes out in shallow trays with the "eyes" uppermost and place in a light, frost-free position to sprout. This process is called "chitting" and is essential for early crops and preferable for the later maincrops. Very soon small, dark green shoots will appear.

CULTIVATION—The ground for potatoes should be well prepared, incorporating a generous supply of organic matter and applying a base dressing of a balanced fertilizer. Early potatoes are planted in rows 60 cm. (24 in.) apart with each potato 30 cm. (12 in.) apart. Planting depth should be about 12.5 cm. (5 in.), so it is easiest to plant them individually with a trowel. Maincrop potatoes need more space with rows 75 cm. (30 in.) and plants 40 cm. (16 in.) apart. Do not remove any of the shoots, which are essential for a sturdy plant and a heavy crop. Planting can take place from mid- spring onwards.

The new shoots are likely to emerge from the soil quite quickly and possibly before the danger of frost has passed. If this is so, start gently earthing up the plants, drawing a little soil over the shoots for protection. Alternatively, with the forecast of a sudden frost, simple protection, such as a plastic flower pot over each plant, just overnight, will help to avoid damage.

When the plants are growing strongly and about 25 cm. (10 in.) high it is time to earth them up properly. Loosen the soil between the rows lightly with a hoe and, using a draw hoe, drag soil across each row making a ridge about 15 cm. (6 in.) high. You can add another dressing of fertilizer at this stage. The new crop of potatoes form very near the surface and earthing up keeps the light away from them, preventing them from going green. In this situation, harvesting simply involves peeling the polythene back. Potatoes should be kept well watered throughout the growing cycle.

HARVESTING—Early crops are ready for harvesting as soon as the flowers start to open. Carefully insert a fork into the side of the row and lever underneath, pulling on the top of the plant at the same time. Most of the potatoes will come out still attached to the plant but the soil should be carefully forked through for loose ones. They should be roughly the size of hen's eggs.

Maincrops will be harvested at the end of the season when the stems (haulms) go yellow and die down. Dig in the same way as earlies. Maincrop potatoes can be stored throughout the winter. After digging, carefully wash and dry the crop and store in a cool, dark, frost-free environment using paper sacks, which allow the potatoes to breathe.

RECOMMENDED FIRST EARLIES
"Accent" AGM—*tasty, newish variety, very early, eelworm and scab resistant*
"Red Duke of York" AGM—*heritage variety, delicious flavor*
RECOMMENDED SECOND EARLIES
"Nadine"—*firm white waxy flesh, high yield, good disease resistance,*
"Edzell Blue"—*beautiful rich purple skins, white flesh and good flavor*
RECOMMENDED MAINCROPS
"Maris Piper"—*excellent yields and a good cooking potato, resistant to eelworm*
"Rooster"—*pink skin, waxy yellow flesh, heavy cropper*
RECOMMENDED SALAD POTATOES
"Anya"—*early, modern version of "pink fir apple," good taste*
"Charlotte"—*early maturing, small, waxy potatoes, good flavor, disease resistant*

PESTS AND DISEASES—Potatoes do suffer from a bewildering range of pests and diseases. Many old allotments or vegetable gardens may well be infected with soil-borne potato cyst eelworms. Growth will be stunted and the yield severely reduced. Always buy good, certified seed potatoes to avoid bringing in this pest. Slugs are also particularly attracted to potatoes and can render the crop totally unusable. They are worse in wet seasons and on heavy soils. Use slug control measures in mid-summer and lift maincrops as soon as possible in the autumn.

Potato Blight
Potato blight is a major problem, causing brown patches on the leaves with moldy edges. It spreads rapidly in damp conditions and will cause the total death of the crop. It is well worthwhile doing a preventative spray for this in mid-summer using a copper fungicide, such as the traditional Bordeaux mixture. As blight tends to strike particularly in late summer, it is worth growing only the quicker maturing, first and second early potato crops rather than maincrops. These are then harvested before blight really appears. A few new varieties, such as "sarpo mira," show some resistance to this disease.

Onion (or allium) family

The onion family includes some valuable and highly flavored vegetables, many of which are available throughout the year. As well as the familiar onions and leeks, there are also salad onions, garlic, shallots, and pickling onions. Apart from garlic, which needs a warm summer, all are easily grown.

Onions

Undoubtedly one of the most useful vegetables in the kitchen, these are used in a host of different dishes. The most widely used onions are the bulb onions available as mild red ones, as well as familiar white ones. Onions can be grown from seeds or from small, immature bulbs called sets, which are easy to grow. Shallots are also planted as bulbs and make a cluster of mild-flavored small bulbs. Japanese onions are sown in late summer and harvested in early summer the following year.

PLANTING SETS—Onion sets are planted in early spring with rows 25 cm. (10 in.) apart and the individual sets 10 cm. (4 in.) apart. Birds are inclined to tug them out by the little whiskery tops, so it is worth trimming these short before planting. Plant with a trowel or small dibber, leaving the top just showing. Shallots are planted in a similar fashion.

SOWING SEEDS Growing onions from seed is a little more difficult. Prepare a fine tilth and sow the seed in drills about 1 cm. (½ in.) deep at the same row spacings as sets. Seed can also be sown earlier in a cool greenhouse, grown in small modules and planted out in mid-spring.

CULTIVATION—Onions like a good, rich, well-drained soil that has been prepared by digging in generous amounts of organic matter. Thin seedlings to 10 cm. (4 in.) apart, when the seedlings are about 5 cm. (2 in.) tall. Keep onion crops well watered and weed free. Remove the flower heads from any bolting plants.

HARVESTING – Onion and shallot crops are usually ready for harvesting around mid- to late summer when the foliage will start to yellow and topple. This can be encouraged by gently folding over the top growth just above the bulb. When the foliage has totally withered, gently loosen the bulbs and lift with a fork. The bulbs should be laid out in a dry, airy location to continue ripening for about two to three weeks. They can then be stored in a cool, frost-free shed for most of the winter. Over the storage months, check the crop and remove any that show signs of rotting.

Garlic

Garlic can also be grown by splitting up the bulbs into the individual scales, which are treated like onion sets. It should be planted in the autumn to give a long growing season.

RECOMMENDED ONIONS FROM SETS
"Sturon" AGM—*flavorsome, medium sized, good keeping qualities*
"Red Baron" AGM—*bright red skin, good flavor, stores well*
RECOMMENDED ONIONS FROM SEEDS
"Ailsa Craig"—*traditional, large bulbs, good for exhibition, limited storage*
"Karmen"—*red-skinned variety, heavy cropper, excellent keeper*
RECOMMENDED SHALLOTS
"Golden Gourmet" AGM—*heavy crops, good flavor, stores well.*
"Jermor" AGM—*great-tasting, pink-tinged flesh, good yield*

PESTS AND DISEASES—Onions suffer from onion fly, which causes yellow drooping leaves. The roots and bulbs will be infested with maggots. Sets are less prone to damage. Eelworm causes twisted, distorted growth, for which there is no cure. White rot causes the bulbs to rot in the soil. With all these problems, destroy any infected plants and grow the crop on fresh soil. Crop rotation is most important to avoid these problems.

Leeks

These are another member of the onion family, grown for their long white "stems" that are produced by either earthing up the crop or by deep planting. They need a long growing season.

SOWING—Sow leeks in a seedbed outside in early spring. Alternatively, plants can also be raised in modules under glass.

CULTIVATION—The young plants should be planted in their final positions in early summer, when they are about 25 cm. (9 in.) tall. They are carefully lifted from the seedbed; the tops and roots are lightly trimmed. Mark out rows about 20 cm. (8 in.) apart and make holes with a dibber about 15 cm. (6 in.) deep. Drop the seedlings in and water to settle the roots. No filling or firming is needed. Keep the crop weeded and well watered. As they grow the plants can be further earthed up to give a greater length of blanched stem.

HARVESTING—Leeks are usually ready for use from mid-autumn onwards and will remain usable in their rows through till early spring the next year.

RECOMMENDED LEEKS
"Carlton" AGM—*recent variety, rapid growth, good flavor, tight stems, stays clean*
"Longbow" AGM—*holds in good condition until spring*
"Armor"—*useful for pulling as mini-leeks*

PESTS AND DISEASES—Leeks suffer from onion flies and eelworm, so crop rotation is recommended with related crops.

Salads

The most traditional ingredient of salads is, of course, lettuce, although there are many others, such as endive, chicory, corn salad, rocket, mustard, and cress. Others may nowadays be sold as packets of mixed seed that can be grown for cutting as tender, young leaves.

Lettuce

These are a relatively easy crop to grow but the trick is maintaining a continuity and variety of this valuable salad. By choosing the right types and using basic protection, lettuce can be produced throughout the year.

The commonest, although probably least attractive, lettuce are the butterhead or roundhead types, which form a round soft heart. Crisphead lettuces are similar but have a crisp center. Cos lettuces have long leaves and are usually fairly crisp. Romaine lettuce are a type of cos. Loose-leaf lettuces are much softer in texture, and useful for just picking a few leaves. There are various fancy leaf types with frilly or oak-leaved foliage and they also come with red leaves, as well as green. Sowing mixed seed gives a variety of salads and also an extended harvesting.

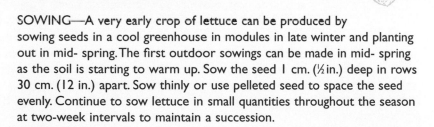

SOWING—A very early crop of lettuce can be produced by sowing seeds in a cool greenhouse in modules in late winter and planting out in mid- spring. The first outdoor sowings can be made in mid- spring as the soil is starting to warm up. Sow the seed 1 cm. (½ in.) deep in rows 30 cm. (12 in.) apart. Sow thinly or use pelleted seed to space the seed evenly. Continue to sow lettuce in small quantities throughout the season at two-week intervals to maintain a succession.

CULTIVATION—Lettuces need a well cultivated soil with an alkaline pH and a high level of organic matter. The use of cloches, a polythene tunnel, or cold frame will ensure an early or late crop. When large enough to handle, thin to 20–30 cm. (8–12 in.) according to the variety and water gently. Young transplants should be planted at the same spacing. To produce lettuce through the winter, you will need a frost-free greenhouse and you must grow very carefully to avoid problems such as damping off (see page 45).

RECOMMENDED BUTTERHEAD TYPES
"Clarion" AGM—*good for early sowing, mildew resistant*
"Tom Thumb"—*early, tiny solid heads, few outer leaves, individual portion size*
RECOMMENDED CRISPHEAD TYPES
"Lakeland" AGM—*good in cooler climates*
"Sioux" AGM—*bronze coloring and good mildew resistance*
RECOMMENDED COS TYPES
"Lobjoits Green Cos" AGM—*traditional variety, firm and crisp, good flavor*
"Little Gem" AGM—*another tiny lettuce, sweet, resistant to root aphid*
RECOMMENDED LOOSE LEAF TYPES
"Catalogna" AGM—*tender leaves, good flavor*
"Lolla Rossa" AGM—*red frilly leaves, tough but pretty as a garnish*
"Delicato" AGM—*very dark purple, oak-leaved lettuce, stands well*
RECOMMENDED OTHER TYPES
"Winter Density" AGM—*hardy lettuce for autumn sowing outdoors*
"Rosetta"—*winter greenhouse lettuce, good flavor, resistant to mildew*

PESTS AND DISEASES—Lettuce are badly attacked by slugs and birds, both of which can decimate the crop. They can also be attacked by ordinary aphid and also lettuce root aphid, which live on the roots but cause the tops to go yellow and wilt. Tipburn shows as brown-edged leaves and is caused by sun scorch. Under glass and particularly during the winter, lettuces are likely to suffer from botrytis and downy mildew. Good ventilation is vital to discourage this.

Salad leaves

As well as lettuce, there are many other edible plants that can be grown for a tasty salad. You can either grow plants close together in rows and cut the young leaves as soon as they are big enough— various mixes are available—or you can select those that you like and sow them at the right season.

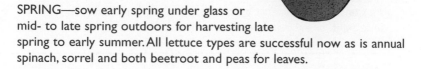

SPRING—sow early spring under glass or mid- to late spring outdoors for harvesting late spring to early summer. All lettuce types are successful now as is annual spinach, sorrel and both beetroot and peas for leaves.

SUMMER—sow late spring to mid-summer for harvesting late spring to late summer. Lettuce can still be sown, and, in addition, endive, chicory, land cress, and East Asian leaves, such as mizuna and mustards can be grown.

AUTUMN—sow mid-summer to early autumn for harvesting mid-autumn to early winter. Endive, chicory, and East Asian leaves still do well at this time of year, as does sweet rocket, leaf radish, and corn salad, otherwise known as lambs lettuce. When sown in late summer this should survive throughout the winter.

WINTER—although some leaves such as lambs lettuce, rocket, mizuna, and spinach will grow and provide leaves during the winter, they are often of poor quality and splashed by mud. A more reliable supply can be obtained by growing these species under glass.

Salad Onions

These are grown from seed with the rows 15 cm. (6 in.) apart. The crop does not need thinning, as onions are pulled young and succulent, as needed. "White Lisbon" AGM is a good white variety and there are those such as "North Holland Blood Red" with red skins.

Mediterranean vegetables

A few vegetables are totally tender and must be raised as young plants under glass before planting outside after all danger of frost has passed. Outside, the soil temperature is rarely high enough in the early part of the year to germinate seed and in order to get a reasonable crop you need a head start with part-grown plants. Interestingly, many are actually fruits but treated as vegetables, as they are used for savory dishes.

Zucchinis

These are like small marrows and in fact the techniques for growing are the same as they are for pumpkins and squashes. Normally, zucchinis form quite tight, bushy plants, whereas the rest are trailing plants that take up a great deal of space.

SOWING—Sow the seeds in a warm greenhouse in mid- to late spring. Plants grow fast so do not sow too early. Use 9 cm. (3½ in.) pots filled with potting compost. Sow two seeds in each pot, pushing them gently into the compost about 2 cm. (1 in.) deep. If both germinate, reduce to one seedling and grow on in a warm, sunny, frost-free greenhouse. Harden off before planting out in early summer.

CULTIVATION—Zucchinis need an open, sunny situation and respond to a deeply cultivated, very rich soil. You should prepare a small pit, partly filled with compost and finished off with topsoil, for each plant. Complete with a base fertilizer and a saucer-like depression around the plant to make watering easy later on. Bush zucchinis should be spaced at least 60 cm. (24 in.) apart and trailing marrows and squashes need to be 1.2 m. (4 ft.) apart. Keep well watered at all times and feed regularly with a high potassium liquid feed, such as a tomato feed.

Zucchinis and marrows all produce separate male and female flowers; you can see the females as they have tiny embryonic fruits behind the flower. These are normally pollinated by insects but if the season is cold it can be helpful to hand pollinate, transferring pollen from the male flower to the female.

HARVESTING—Zucchinis must be picked very frequently, when the fruits are about 10 cm. (4 in.) long. They are best used fresh but can be sliced and frozen. If harvesting is delayed, zucchinis rapidly grow into marrows and production slows down. Some people find the prickly leaves an irritant, so you may wish to harvest zucchinis wearing gloves and a long sleeved shirt. Incidentally, the male flowers are also edible and can be deep fried as a tasty delicacy.

RECOMMENDED ZUCCHINIS, MARROWS AND SQUASHES

"Defender" AGM—*early, compact, heavy-cropping zucchini, resistant to virus*
"Firenze" AGM—*high yield, resistant to mildew and less spiny so easy to harvest*
"Soleil"—*golden yellow zucchini, heavy cropping, mildew tolerant*
"Sunburst" AGM—*golden patty pan-style squash to eat small, great taste*
"Tiger Cross" AGM—*grow for either zucchinis or marrows, virus resistant*
"Cobnut"—*butternut squash, good crop, full flavor*
"Hundredweight"—*traditional Halloween-style giant pumpkin, trailing*

PESTS AND DISEASES—They are very prone to slug damage, so use protection as soon as planted. In a warm summer they may suffer from whitefly and viruses sometimes appear, which check growth of the crop. Zucchinis may be attacked by mildew. Avoid this by growing a resistant variety and keeping crops well watered.

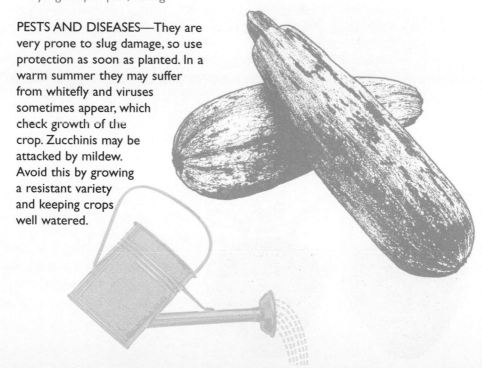

Sweetcorn

This highly flavored and sweeter version of maize needs a warm summer to perform at its best. Some of the more recent F1 hybrids have been bred to respond better to cooler climates. The extra sweet ones should be grown away from standard types as cross-pollination reduces the sweetness.

SOWING—Sow the seed in mid- to late spring in 9 cm. (3½ in.) pots of good potting compost, placing two seeds about 2 cm. (1 in.) deep and lightly covering. Germinate in a warm greenhouse and then grow on in good light. Remove the weaker of the two seedlings if both germinate. Harden off before planting out after all danger of frost has passed in early summer.

CULTIVATION—The site for sweetcorn should be warm and sunny with a well-drained soil, prepared in the normal way. Plants have separate male and female flowers and are wind pollinated. Male flowers are large, decorative tassels at the top of the plants. Female flowers that will lead to cobs are lower down. Sweetcorn is best grown in a block to encourage pollination. Space the plants about 45 cm. (18 in.) square, watering in well after planting. Keep free of weeds and water in dry weather.

HARVESTING—Each plant will produce two to three cobs, which normally ripen in late summer and early autumn. The remains of the female flowers are called "silks" and start to turn brown as the crop is ripening. Gently peel back the green outer sheath and press into a kernel with a fingernail. If the fluid appears milky rather than clear, then the cob is ripe and ready to harvest. They are best fresh but can be frozen for winter use.

RECOMMENDED SWEETCORN

"Sundance" AGM—*early, reliable, long cobs, good in cooler summers*
"Swift" AGM—*very early, vigorous, very sweet, good on cold soils*

PESTS AND DISEASES—Relatively free from diseases, may suffer slug damage.

Outdoor tomatoes
These are a bit of a gamble in cooler climates, although given a sheltered spot and a reasonable summer, some useful later fruit can be grown, usually with excellent flavor. Outdoor varieties of tomatoes should be specifically selected.

SOWING—Start the seeds in mid- spring and produce plants as for glasshouse types (see pages 120–123)

CULTIVATION—Prepare a well-drained soil patch with generous dressings of organic matter in the standard way. Prior to planting, harden off carefully. Both types are planted 45 cm. (18 in.) apart with rows 90 cm. (3 ft.) apart.

Bush types do not need pinching or staking. Tie cordon types to a 1.5 m. (5 ft.) cane as they grow. Remove side shoots, as you would with greenhouse tomatoes. Pinch out the growing point after the fourth truss, as this is likely to be all that the plant can ripen in a cool climate outdoors.

Keep weed free, water, and feed regularly. As fruit develops, spread a mulch of straw to keep the fruit off the ground. Also apply slug protection.

HARVESTING—Pick the fruits as they ripen. At the end of the season, before the frosts, pick all remaining fruit. These should be placed in an enclosed area, such as a drawer, with a ripe apple, which encourages ripening.

RECOMMENDED OUTDOOR TOMATOES
"Roma VF"—*heavy cropping, plum-shaped fruits, almost seedless, excellent*
"Marmande" AGM—*huge, beefsteak style tomato, very fleshy, excellent for slicing*
"Tornado" AGM—*early, compact, good for cool summer, sweet, heavy crop*

PESTS AND DISEASES—Outdoor tomatoes suffer from similar pests and diseases to greenhouse ones but probably to a lesser extent. Potato blight is particularly troublesome if potatoes are growing nearby.

Celery

Traditionally, celery was a very tedious vegetable to produce, requiring growing in a trench, and then earthing up the plants to create tender white stems. Modern, self-blanching types do away with the need for this, but the taste is possibly inferior.

SOWING—Start the seed under heated glass in early spring and prick off seedlings into trays or small modules. Grow cool and harden off before planting out in late spring.

CULTIVATION—The site should be open and sunny and prepared in the normal way. Plant the seedlings 25 cm. (9 in.) apart in blocks, as the close proximity of neighboring plants will assist the blanching process. Keep well watered and weed-free.

HARVESTING—They should be ready for use from late summer but the self-blanching types are not hardy so must be harvested before the autumn frosts.

RECOMMENDED CELERY
"Loretta" AGM—*self-blanching, vigorous, excellent flavor, white sticks*
"Golden Self-blanching"—*very early, compact, crisp heads*

PESTS AND DISEASES—Celery may be attacked by slugs and also by celery fly, a type of leaf miner causing brown blisters on the leaves.

Spinach and chard

True spinach is a fast-growing annual vegetable, sometimes with a strong flavor, best picked when tender and young. For those that find annual spinach difficult to grow, you can try perpetual spinach, also known as leaf beet, which is similar but does not run to seed and will grow on through the season and into the winter. It is not so tender or delicate flavored. There are also the colored chards or leaf beets, such as "ruby chard" which are very ornamental but are grown and cooked in a similar way.

SOWING—Sow annual spinach from early spring onwards for cropping from early summer. Repeat sowings at monthly intervals to provide a succession of young leaves. Space rows about 30 cm. (12 in.) apart, sow sparingly in 2.5 cm. (1 in.) drills. Sow perpetual spinach in mid-summer for an autumn and winter crop.

CULTIVATION—As this is a leafy crop, the soil should be well prepared with generous amounts of organic matter and base fertilizer. You should thin seedlings to 7.5 cm. (3 in.) apart. It does not perform well in hot, dry summers, as it tends to run to seed too quickly, so keep the crop adequately watered.

HARVESTING—Pick individual leaves when young, or cut the whole plant to a stump, which will often re-sprout with a second flush of growth.

RECOMMENDED SPINACH AND CHARD
"Scenic" AGM—*high yielding, full flavored, downy mildew resistant*
"Mikado"—*highly productive, slow to bolt, resistant to downy mildew*
"Perpetual Spinach" AGM (Leaf Beet)—*hardy, good for a winter crop*
"Bright Lights" AGM (Chard)—*multicolored leaf stems, mild sweet flavor*

PESTS AND DISEASES—Spinach plants tend to be relatively free from pests and diseases. Yellow leaves can indicate either a manganese deficiency or downy mildew. With the latter, there will be a gray mold on the underside of the leaves.

Asparagus
This is a perennial crop that can be productive for many years once it is established. The edible parts are the plump young stems, as they push through the ground in spring and early summer. These are called spears.

PLANTING—Asparagus can be grown from seed but obtaining young plants will save time. Buy one-year-old crowns, which will have been grown from seed. These are quite cumbersome plants with wide-spreading thongy roots. Never let them dry out while waiting to plant. As the crop will be in place for many years, make a particular effort to thoroughly prepare the soil, ideally by double digging, incorporating generous amounts of organic matter.

Plant asparagus in winter, while the roots are still dormant. Take out a trench that is about 15 cm. (6 in.) deep and 30 cm. (12 in.) wide, leaving a slight mound in the center. Spread the roots out about 40 cm. (15 in.) apart. Carefully cover with about 5 cm. (2 in.) of fine topsoil, which will leave the crowns to grow in a shallow trench.

CULTIVATION—During the first season, keep the area carefully weeded and regularly watered. As the asparagus "fern" grows, gently replace the remaining soil back into the trench around the asparagus plants until it is level by autumn. When the foliage yellows in the autumn, cut down to about 5 cm. (2 in.). During subsequent years, apply a general fertilizer in early spring and rake or hoe into the surface. Earth up each plant lightly using a draw hoe. This will increase the length of the white spear.

HARVESTING—This can take place from the second year onwards in mid-spring. Cut the spears when they are about 10–12.5 cm., (4–5 in.) above ground. Use a serrated-bladed knife to sever them about 7.5 cm. (3 in.) below ground. Stop cutting by early summer to let the foliage grow and allow the plant to build up its strength for the next season.

RECOMMENDED ASPARAGUS
"Connovers Colossal" AGM—*early, good quality, reliable*
"Gijnlim" AGM—*all male variety, early, heavy cropping*

PESTS AND DISEASES—Asparagus suffers from slugs, which eat the young spears. Later in the season, asparagus beetles, which have distinctive black and orange bodies with white blotches, feed on the foliage. They can be controlled by spraying.

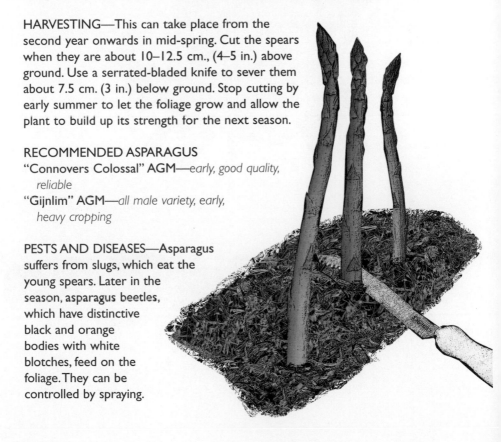

Growing fruit

Most fruits are long-term plants and often do not come into full cropping for a number of years. For this reason they are probably better planted in your own garden than on a rented allotment. Some, such as pears, are attractive garden plants with bold shapes, pretty spring blossoms and good autumn color, so any fruit could be considered a bonus.

Types of fruit

Fruit is generally divided into top fruit and soft fruit. Top fruits are the tree fruits, such as apple, pear, plum, and cherry, with the possible addition of apricots, peaches, nectarines, and figs, which are usually grown with the protection of a wall or under glass. Soft fruits include gooseberries, white currants, red- and blackcurrants, raspberries, blackberries and loganberries and, of course, strawberries. There are also other fruits, including hybrid berries such as tayberries and blueberries, which are becoming popular, and specialist fruits, such as kiwis and grapes.

Fruit basics

All fruits require thorough soil preparation in advance of planting. Any perennial weeds should be cleared using glyphosate or alternative treatment, such as described on page 28. Dig the soil thoroughly, incorporating generous quantities of organic matter. Most fruits are best planted during the winter dormant season, although you may be able to obtain pot-grown plants from garden centers during the spring and summer. You will need to ensure that these are kept well watered during their first season. With tree fruits, you can either buy a small "maiden" tree, which will need training into the desired shape, or you can obtain older, partly trained trees, which have already had some formative pruning and training

During the winter, young trees and bushes will usually be bare-frooted and it is essential that these roots are not allowed to dry out. Dig a hole that is large enough to accommodate the roots without cramping. Mix a high phosphate fertilizer, such as bonemeal with the spare soil and into the base of the hole. Spread out the roots and gently refill the soil, firming it in with your boots. Most fruit trees will benefit from a stake to support them in the first few years. With a bare root tree, it is best to put the stake in the hole before the tree, so that you don't damage the roots when you drive it in. With pot-grown trees, use a short stake and angle it across the stem and away from the root ball. Use a proper rubber tree tie to secure the tree or alternatively a pair of old tights.

Fruit bushes are planted in a similar way but do not normally need staking. Most fruit trees and bushes benefit from fairly hard pruning immediately after planting. This will encourage strong new healthy growth during the first season, after the new roots have established. Keep new fruit trees well watered, ideally with a mulch to retain soil moisture. Keep free of weeds during the early years and check regularly for pests and diseases.

During the second and subsequent years, you will need to prune the trees. The methods of doing so are described with the various crops. Feeding can be with a balanced fertilizer, such as Growmore, at 60 g./m.^{2} (2 oz./square yards) during the second year to encourage sturdy growth. As the trees go into their fruiting cycle, this can change to a feed with a higher potassium level, such as sulphate of potassium, which encourages fruit growth.

Top Fruit

Consider the space available for growing tree fruits. A full-size apple tree will take up a great deal of space and may not come into cropping for many years. Fortunately, there are ways of producing small trees by grafting onto dwarfing rootstocks, so always check on the rootstock when buying a fruit tree. Most fruit trees can also be grown in a number of shapes. Trained trees, such as cordons, take up very little space and, when coupled with a dwarfing rootstock, enable fresh fruit to be produced in a small garden.

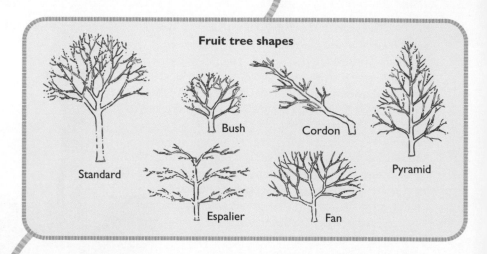

Fruit tree shapes

Standard

Bush

Cordon

Pyramid

Espalier

Fan

Fan, espalier or cordon trees are particularly useful if you have spare wall space to use. Bush and standards generally take up the most space and are really only used if you have space to grow a traditional orchard. Pyramids and cordons are very good for a small garden and take up little space.

Apples

Apples are divided into cooking and eating apples, and there is an extensive choice, particularly of the latter. Some wonderfully flavored apples are available to grow that you will never find in the supermarkets.

PLANTING APPLES—Apple trees are always grafted onto a rootstock, as they do not grow well on their own roots. The stock will govern the eventual size of the tree and the speed of cropping. It is very important to choose an apple on the right rootstock for your garden. Rootstocks also govern other things, such as disease resistance. A good reliable nursery will always state the rootstock for fruit trees but cheap deals may be grafted on anything and this may not be declared or accurate.

ROOTSTOCKS AND THEIR EFFECTS

Rootstock	Description	Height	Cropping	Spacing
M27	Extremely dwarfing	1.5–1.8 m. (5–6 ft.)	2–3 years	0.9–1.2 m. (3–4 ft.)
M9	Very dwarfing	2.4–3.8 m. (8–10 ft.)	3–4 years	1.2–2.4 m. (4–8 ft.)
M26	Dwarfing	3–3.6 m. (10–12 ft.)	3–4 years	2.4–3.6 m. (8–12 ft.)
MM106	Vigorous	4.3–5.5 m. (14–18 ft.)	4–5 years	3.6–4.8 m. (12–16 ft.)
MM111 and M2	Very vigorous	5.5–7.6 m. (18–25 ft.)	6–7 years	4.3–7.6 m. (14–18 ft.)

So there are three initial decisions to make: the rootstock, the shape in which you are going to train your tree and the variety of fruit that you want. When choosing fruit varieties, it is necessary to choose ones that will pollinate each other. Without pollination, fruit will not form so this means that your trees need to flower at the same time. Reliable fruit catalogs will group together the varieties according to pollination needs and flowering times.

PRUNING APPLES—Young apple trees are pruned fairly hard for the first few years, removing a third to a half of the new growth, always back to a bud that is pointing away from the center of the tree. Pruning normally takes place during the winter dormant period. Generally, remove dead, diseased, or damaged wood and keep the tree open, avoiding over-crowding. Trees, such as cordons, that are being trained to wires on a wall must be tied in, ideally as they are growing during the summer, before the shoots harden.

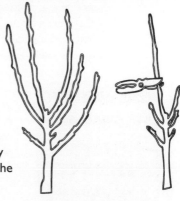

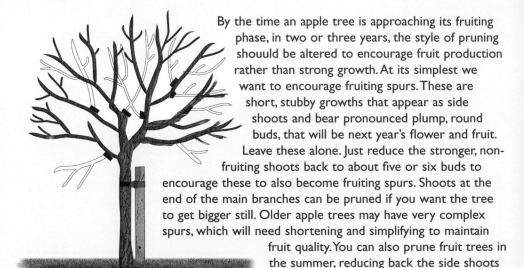

By the time an apple tree is approaching its fruiting phase, in two or three years, the style of pruning shouuld be altered to encourage fruit production rather than strong growth. At its simplest we want to encourage fruiting spurs. These are short, stubby growths that appear as side shoots and bear pronounced plump, round buds, that will be next year's flower and fruit. Leave these alone. Just reduce the stronger, non-fruiting shoots back to about five or six buds to encourage these to also become fruiting spurs. Shoots at the end of the main branches can be pruned if you want the tree to get bigger still. Older apple trees may have very complex spurs, which will need shortening and simplifying to maintain fruit quality. You can also prune fruit trees in the summer, reducing back the side shoots to three or four leaves to encourage these to become fruiting spurs.

POLLINATION AND FRUIT THINNING—Flowering time is a very critical season for fruit crops and a late frost can destroy all the blossom or tiny fruits and result in a partial or total crop failure. If a frost is predicted, smaller trees can be protected sufficiently with a layer of horticultural fleece or old net curtains. If pollination and fruit set is successful, you can sometimes have an excess of fruit that will never mature properly. A natural drop occurs during early summer, so wait until after that and then thin the young fruitlets to one per cluster.

HARVESTING AND STORAGE—Fruit is ripe when you gently lift an apple and the stem parts easily. Some types of apple will store well into the winter in a cool, dark shed, or garage. Wrapping in greaseproof paper or in perforated polythene bags will help to avoid shrinkage.

RECOMMENDED EARLY FLOWERING APPLES
"Egremont Russet" AGM—*rough skin, sweet nutty flesh, lovely old apple*
"Rev W Wilks"—*a good, compact cooking apple, but a biennial bearer*
RECOMMENDED MID-SEASON FLOWERING APPLES
"Discovery" AGM—*one of the best and earliest dessert apples, doesn't keep*
"Cox's Orange Pippin"—*well known but difficult to grow well*
"Fiesta" AGM—*good substitute for "cox," reliable, reasonable flavor*
"Katy"—*modern variety, good cropping, juicy, refreshing*
"James Grieve" AGM—*a good pollinator, early cooker, or dessert apple, when ripe*
"Bramley Seedling" AGM—*the best of cooking apples but a huge spreading tree*
RECOMMENDED LATE FLOWERING APPLES
"Chivers Delight"—*a lovely but rarely grown apple*
"Pixie"—*prolific cropping, disease resistant, small, crisp, juicy fruit*

PESTS AND DISEASES—Apples suffer from a bewildering array of pests and diseases. Various caterpillars and sawflies eat the foliage and flowers, and some burrow into the fruit, causing the typical maggoty fruit. Codling moth can be deterred by using pheromone traps in the trees in spring.

Mildew and scab diseases affect the foliage and weaken growth. Mildew can be reduced by summer pruning and removing infected shoots. Both can be controlled by fungicidal sprays applied as a protection. Brown rot affects many types of fruit, especially in wet summers. Remove any diseased fruit to prevent it spreading. In particular, infected fruit remains on the tree in a mummified form over winter and, if not removed, will start the infection next year.

For good-quality fruit, it is necessary to spray repeatedly throughout the season using a mixture of fungicides and insecticides. Spray about every two weeks from leaf burst through until mid-summer, avoiding blossom time. If you do not like the idea of spraying regularly, don't spray at all but allow the natural balance of predators and parasites to develop. Fruit will not be perfect but some crop should be possible.

Pears

The culture of pears is very similar to that of apples. Pear trees can be trained in a range of shapes and the general planting, formative pruning and routine culture is similar to that of apples. In general, pears like a warmer location than apples and prefer a heavier soil, although good drainage is essential.

PLANTING PEARS—The choice of rootstocks for pears is much simpler: Quince A makes a medium-sized tree and Quince C makes a dwarf tree. Pears also require a compatible pollinator and this can be complicated, as there are some that are totally incompatible, even though they may flower at the same time.

PRUNING PEARS—Routine pruning is similar to that of apples, although they will tolerate harder pruning. Pears tend to produce copious spurs and so spur thinning on older trees is essential to maintain fruit quality and vigor.

HARVESTING AND STORAGE—Early pears must be picked and eaten as soon as they are ripe. Ideally, pick them slightly prematurely and ripen them indoors. Watch for a slight lightening of the skin color and check to see if the stalk parts easily from the tree. If left too long the fruit loses its delicate flavor and the flesh becomes brown and mushy, described as "sleepy." Before eating, bring the fruit into a warm room for a couple of days to allow the full flavors to develop.

RECOMMENDED EARLY FLOWERING PEARS
"William's Bon Chretien" AGM—*good early cropper, disease resistant, will not store*
"Conference"—*easy, partly self-fertile, hardy but susceptible to scab*

RECOMMENDED LATE FLOWERING PEARS
"'Doyenne du Comice" AGM—*exquisite fruit, but difficult and irregular cropper*
"Concorde" AGM—*recent introduction, reliable, heavy cropping, good flavor*
"Beth" AGM—*another new one, heavy cropping, superb texture and flavor*

PESTS AND DISEASES—Pears are affected by similar pests and diseases to
apples, plus the pear midge, which causes fruitlets to go black and drop off.
Always destroy any fallen fruitlets before the maggots enter the soil and
pupate. Also, keep the soil under the trees loosely cultivated to encourage
birds to forage and eat the grubs. You can also spray for this pest.

Plums

These are classed as stone fruits, and are some of the most succulent fruit
available in temperate gardens. Gages and damsons also come within this
group. Plum trees are not particularly fussy but succeed best on a warm,
sheltered site with a well-drained, moisture retentive soil. Some are self-
fertile so you may not need a pollinator.

PLANTING—Soil preparation and planting are the same as for planting
any other tree fruit. Plums are most often grown as bushes, half standards
and sometimes as fan-trained trees. The most suitable rootstock for plums
is "pixie," which makes a very dwarf tree with a mature height of around
3 m. (10 ft.). "St Julien A," which is semi-dwarfing stock, is a
better choice than "pixie" if conditions
are not ideal.

PRUNING—Young plum trees
are pruned to encourage three
to five strong main branches.
Plum trees produce fruit on
spurs, on two-year-old wood and
sometimes at the base of one-year
wood so pruning is similar to that of apples
and pears. The most critical thing to

remember is that you should always prune plums during the summer. This is because plums are very susceptible to silver leaf disease, which is more readily transmitted in the winter. Any major pruning cuts should also be treated with an arboricultural paint to seal them.

ROUTINE CARE—Mulch annually and feed with a balanced general fertilizer in early spring. Plums flower quite early and the blossom can be damaged by frost. If frost is forecast and trees are small enough, protect blossom or young fruitlets with fleece or old net curtains. Keep well watered when the fruit is developing.

RECOMMENDED EARLY FLOWERING PLUMS
"Victoria" AGM psf—*best known plum, reliable and heavy cropping, but prone to disease*
"Opal" AGM sf—*early cropping desert plum, easy to grow and good flavor*
RECOMMENDED LATE FLOWERING PLUMS
"Oullin's Golden Gage" AGM sf—*an exquisite golden plum, reasonably healthy*
"Cambridge Gage" AGM psf—*a traditional green gage, juicy, good flavor, reliable*
"Czar" AGM sf—*purple plum, tangy yellow flesh, cooks well, regular cropping*

sf = self fertile, psf = partially self fertile

PESTS AND DISEASES—Silver leaf disease is the main problem. Leaves on affected plants appear silvery white and almost translucent. The fungus will spread throughout the tree and from tree to tree. It transmits via open wounds and pruning cuts. If just a small part of the tree appears to be infected, prune those branches out, cutting at least 12 cm. (5 in.) beyond where the symptoms are showing. Infected wood is stained brown in the center. Bacterial canker shows as cankers on the stems that ooze. Aphids and winter moth caterpillars may also attack plums. When the fruit is ripening, wasps can be a major problem, feeding on the fruit and becoming a hazard to pickers.

Cherries

These are not a widely grown crop in private gardens, as the trees tend to be large. The newer, dwarfing rootstock "Gisella 5" or the older "colt" do make cherry growing more feasible, although they are still large trees for a relatively small crop. The variety "stella" is a good one for the private garden, as it is self-fertile and produces sweet, juicy fruits. "Morello" is a good self-fertile cooking cherry that grows well as a fan-trained tree. Pruning is similar to plums. Cherries also suffer from silver leaf disease, so prune these in the summer too.

Peaches and nectarines

These like a warm, sheltered location so are best grown against a sunny wall as fan trained trees. They are fussy plants and so you need to be prepared to give extra attention and despite this, a good crop is only likely in warm summers. When successful, however, home-grown fruit can be exquisite. They fruit on last year's wood so prune out a proportion of old wood each year to encourage new growth and tie this in as the season develops. If frost threatens, be sure to protect the early blossom using fleece or old net curtains. "Duke of York" and "Rochester" are good peaches and "early rivers" is a good nectarine. One of the biggest problems with these fruits is peach leaf curl, although there are some new resistant varieties such as the peach "avalon pride," which are less likely to be infected.

Soft fruit

This is a wide group of fruits, so named because of their soft skins. They are all relatively low growing and can be looked after and harvested from ground level. Because they are a wide group, there are many variations in their culture. Soft fruit is not difficult to grow but will not perform well if neglected, so be prepared to make an investment of time in order to reap a good crop.

Buying Healthy Stock

All soft fruits, and particularly strawberries, suffer from many pests and diseases, especially viruses. Specialist producers grow stock that is certified as totally healthy. You should always buy good, certified stock from a reputable nursery. If your own plants appear to be healthy and crop well, you can propagate these, although it is wise to buy in new fresh stock every few years. Do not be tempted to buy or accept stocks from an unknown source.

Strawberries

Growing your own strawberries gives you the opportunity to grow some of the better-flavored varieties that are often not sold in the shops. This wonderful fruit gives worthwhile crops for three years maximum, after which they should be discarded. It is a very rewarding crop giving the biggest and best quality fruit in the year after planting. The heavier yield of smaller fruits is in the second year, tailing off in the third.

PLANTING STRAWBERRIES—Strawberries like an open, sunny site, with some shelter. They will grow on most soils, provided they are well drained, but prefer a slightly acid soil. Prepare the site by digging and incorporating organic matter and a base fertilizer dressing just before planting. If you have room for three rows of strawberries, replant one row each year. Ideally you should plant the new row in a different location to the old one as some strawberry pests and diseases are soil-borne.

Unlike most fruits, the best time to plant strawberries is in mid- to late summer, which will result in a full crop the following year. If you plant in spring, the flowers must be removed to avoid cropping the same season. Don't be tempted to leave them on! Plant strawberries shallowly, 45 cm. (18 in.) apart in rows 75 cm. (30 in.) apart. Finish off by firming in and watering. During the rest of the first season, keep watered and weed free. The plants may produce runners, which are long, waving shoots that the plant uses to replicate itself. At this stage remove these.

CULTIVATION—During the following spring, apply sulphate of potassium at 30 g./m.² (1 oz./square yards) and rake or hoe into the surface. At the same time, tidy up the plants, removing any of last year's leaves that have died. As the weather warms up, the plants will burst into fresh growth and by mid to late spring, flowers will appear. Mulch the plants with clean straw, which will not only retain moisture but keep the fruit from getting muddy. Water frequently as the fruit develops and ripens. When cropping has finished, the plants can be trimmed back and old foliage, runners, and the straw removed. Apply a general balanced fertilizer and water well to start back into fresh growth and build up the plants ready for the next year.

Strawberries grow well in containers. You can use ordinary flower pots, traditional strawberry pots that have several holes in the sides or growbags. Position the latter on a support off the ground, to allow the fruit to hang down cleanly. In this way, the fruit will avoid damage from slugs and soiling with mud.

PROPAGATING STRAWBERRIES—If strawberry plants are healthy you can propagate your own. In early summer look for healthy strong runners and pin these down into small

pots of potting compost plunged alongside the mother plants. Keep the pots moist and in about four or five weeks the runners will have rooted and can be severed from the mother plant. Remove any extension runner that may also be present on the new plants. These can be planted out almost straight away in mid to late summer.

HARVESTING—Wait until the fruit is fully colored and pick daily during the cropping season. The fruit is picked by gently cupping in the palm and pinching the stalk so that the fruit is harvested with its stalk. Handle very gently at all times. Pick all ripe fruits and discard any damaged ones. Damaged fruit left on the plant will encourage disease.

RECOMMENDED STRAWBERRIES
"Honeoye" AGM—*good early cropping variety, bright red fruits*
"Hapil" AGM—*good flavor, high yields, does well in light soils and dry seasons*
"Cambridge Favorite" AGM—*mid-season, a reliable high cropper but tasteless!*
"Aromel" AGM—*a perpetual fruiting type with good flavor*
"Mara des Bois"—*taste of wild strawberry, good sized fruit, long cropping period*
"Elsanta"—*mid season, wonderful flavor and high yields but prone to disease*

Early Strawberries in Polytunnels

A valuable early crop of strawberries can be produced using the protection of a low polythene tunnel. You will need a row of healthy strawberry plants, established from runners planted the previous summer. In late winter or early spring, cover the row with a low polythene tunnel. These are fabricated from semi-circular hoops of stiff wire covered with a canopy of polythene held on with a thinner wire loop. The polythene is anchored in the soil at each end of the row but the sides are free and can be raised for ventilation and eventually picking. Raise the sides when the strawberries are flowering to allow for pollination. Ripening can be several weeks in advance of unprotected crops.

PESTS AND DISEASES—Strawberry fruit is very prone to damage by birds and slugs as it ripens. Netting must be used to keep birds away and some form of slug protection is essential. Strawberries are prone to attack by aphids, which transmit viruses, and occasionally by red spider mite. In damp seasons, the fruit may be attacked by gray mould and rot. Remove and burn any affected fruit as soon as it is seen. Red core is a serious soil-borne disease that causes the plant to collapse. Destroy the plants and grow strawberries on a fresh site.

Raspberries

This fruit grows better in cool conditions and as it flowers later, is less likely to be damaged by frost. The fruit is borne on woody stems called canes. Each cane lasts two years making most of its growth from the ground in the first season and then fruiting in the second, before dying.

PLANTING RASPBERRIES—Raspberries can remain productive for at least five years, so good thorough preparation with plenty of organic matter is advisable. The canes are not self-supporting, so need a framework of posts and wire. Use 2.4 m. (8 ft.) tree stakes, driven in the ground at each end of the row and if the row is longer than 3 m. (10 ft.), add intermediate posts. Stretch three galvanized wires between the posts at 75 cm. (30 in.), 1.2 m. (4 ft.) and 1.6 m. (5ft. 6 in.) above the ground. These will not be needed until growth is vigorous but it is easiest to construct the frame before planting.

Raspberry canes are best planted when dormant in the winter, spacing them between 30–45 cm. (12–18 in.) apart. The closer spacing will require more canes but achieve a bigger crop quicker. Further rows should be spaced 1.8 m. (6 ft.) apart. Plant them along the row, spreading out the fibrous roots, immediately under the wires. When you buy raspberry canes they will usually have already been shortened to about 30–45 cm. (12–18 in.). In early spring of the first year, further prune them back to about 15 cm. (6 in.). This will stimulate the production of a number of young, vigorous shoots, which will be your fruiting canes for next year.

ROUTINE CARE—During the first season, keep the young canes weed free and well watered. A general fertilizer should be applied in early spring of the second year and subsequent years. As the canes grow they can be tied in to the wires with polypropylene string, aiming for canes no closer than 10 cm. (4 in.) apart. Alternatively, you can use short proprietary wire ties but be careful not to strangle the cane. Any canes that grow beyond the top wire should be tipped back at the end of the season. During the period between flowering and fruiting, keep the plants well watered to ensure that the fruit swells correctly. Mulching will help retain moisture and deter weeds.

PRUNING AND TRAINING—After cropping, the first batch of canes will start to die and a further batch of new canes will be pushing up from ground level. Pruning can take place in late summer but most gardeners find it easier to wait until winter and prune during the dormant season. At this stage, all the old fruited canes are pruned out to ground level together with any weak or distorted canes. The new canes are then tied in aiming for a spacing of 10 cm. (4 in.).

This time an easy way to do this job is to use a running string, anchored at the end of the row, working along the bottom wire first. Select a suitable cane, position it against the wire and wrap the string around the cane, then loop around the wire and proceed on to the next cane. Repeat the process for the middle and top wire. In a good plantation there will be surplus canes and all the remaining unwanted canes are then cut out to ground level. Alternatively, unwanted canes can be gently dug up as new stock for a fresh plantation.

HARVESTING—Raspberries are ripened on the plant so must be handled very carefully, plucking the fruit and leaving the plug and stalk. Handle with great care at all times.

Autumn-fruiting Raspberries

Most raspberries fruit in early summer but there are some that crop in the autumn on the current year's canes. They are pruned hard in the spring and the vigorous new canes generally do not require support. Otherwise, they need similar conditions. They produce a very worthwhile crop at a useful time of the year.

RECOMMENDED RASPBERRIES

"Glen Moy" AGM—*compact, well flavored large berries*
"Glen Prosen" AGM—*widely grown, mid-season cropping, good flavor*
"Autumn Bliss" AGM—*good autumn variety, good flavor, heavy cropper*
"Allgold"—*a golden autumn-fruiting raspberry, great taste*

PESTS AND DISEASES—Birds attack the fruit, making it essential to net the crop. Raspberry beetle causes the typical maggoty fruit and must be controlled by spraying when the young fruit is just turning pink. In a wet season, the fruit may become infected with botrytis and start to rot. Spur blight and cane blight can cause die-back of the canes.

Blackberries and hybrid berries

This includes loganberries, tayberries, and a host of other less common fruits such as the boysenberry and Japanese wineberry. They all produce fruit on long whippy canes, which fruit in their second year then die.

PLANTING AND CULTIVATION—Prepare the ground thoroughly and plant during winter, spacing them at least 1.8 m. (6 ft.) apart with a similar distance between rows. Compared to raspberries, they have a more rampant and straggling habit, most with vicious thorns. They need to be trained to wires or a support to make them manageable and for the fruit to be accessible. Posts and wires, as described for raspberries, are suitable but with horizontal wires about 30 cm. (1 ft.) apart. The long whippy canes are tied in and trained horizontally along the wires as they grow. If there are more canes than wires, several canes can be tied at each level.

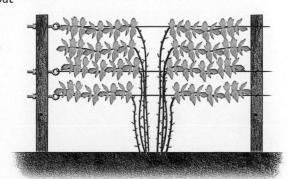

After fruiting, the old fruited canes are cut out and the new young ones trained in. During the summer growing season the new canes can be loosely looped in to prevent damage and then finally trained in position after the previous year's canes are removed. Otherwise, culture is similar to that of raspberries.

PROPAGATION—All theses berries can be propagated by tip layering. This involves burying the tip of a growing shoot in summer. Roots will form and a new shoot will develop. When established, this can be severed from the parent plant and transplanted to a new location.

RECOMMENDED BERRIES
"Black Butte"—*recent introduction, huge berries, good flavor*
"Loch Ness" AGM—*compact, thornless, large fruit*
"Loganberry LY654" AGM—*thornless, original hybrid berry, sharp taste, good for cooking*
"Tayberry Medana"—*thornless, better and sweeter than loganberry, crops well*
"Japanese Wineberry"—*more of an ornamental but with a red fruit, low yields*

PESTS AND DISEASES—These fruits also suffer from raspberry beetle, bird damage, and botrytis.

Blackcurrants

Blackcurrants are an easy and valuable crop to grow giving heavy yields but the bushes are large so they need plenty of space. The fruit is grown almost solely for cooking or preserving and is generally too sharp to be used fresh. The Jostaberry is a hybrid between gooseberry and blackcurrant with large black berries and is an improvement on the earlier Worcesterberry.

PLANTING—Choose an open, sunny, sheltered site and prepare the ground in the normal way. Blackcurrants are best planted as dormant bushes in the winter. One- or two-year-old bushes are usually available. Plant them 1.2–1.5 m. (4–5 ft.) apart, burying the roots about 5 cm. (2 in.) deeper than they were previously growing. You can usually see a soil mark on the stem to give an indication of this. After planting, prune hard back to about 5 cm. (2 in.) above ground level to encourage strong new growth.

CULTIVATION—During the first season, keep weed free and watered during dry spells. Additional feeding during early summer will encourage strong growth. At the end of the first season, little pruning is needed, although any weak shoots, crossed or damaged growths should be removed back to ground level.

PRUNING—Established blackcurrant bushes will need pruning every year. This can take place in late summer after the fruit has been picked or can be left until winter when the structure of the bush is more easily discerned. Each year you should aim to cut out between 25–30% of the older fruited stems. Although individual stems will fruit for a number of years, the younger stems give better quality and higher yields. Old wood can be recognized as it is darker, almost blackish-brown in color. Removing old stems encourages a succession of young growths from ground level. You should also remove low-growing, crossing, damaged or weak growths.

HARVESTING—The first crop will come in the second season. Blackcurrants come in long clusters called "strigs," which should be picked when the majority of the fruit is ripe. Some growers choose to prune at the same time as harvesting by cutting out all the older shoots bearing fruit which can then be processed indoors.

PROPAGATION—Blackcurrants can be easily propagated by 25 cm. (9 in.) hardwood cuttings of one-year shoots taken in the autumn. Be sure that you only propagate from healthy, heavy cropping bushes. You can even plant a group of three cuttings where you want a new bush to grow and avoid the need for transplanting later.

RECOMMENDED BLACKCURRANTS

"Ben Lomond" AGM—*compact plant, heavy crop, later flowering, disease resistant*
"Ben Connan" AGM—*early ripening, heavy crops, pest and disease resistant*
"Jostaberry"—*heavy yield, pleasant flavor, pest and disease resistant*

PESTS AND DISEASES—Blackcurrants suffer from aphids, winter moth caterpillars, and bird damage. They are also prone to big bud mite, which causes large round distorted buds that do not develop. This mite also spreads reversion disease, causing distorted leaves. Remove and burn infected branches and, if necessary, whole bushes.

Redcurrants and White Currants

Although less commonly grown, these are very pleasant and easily grown summer fruits. Both are sweeter than blackcurrants and so can be served fresh, as well as being used for cooking or preserving.

PLANTING—There is no certification scheme but nevertheless aim to buy healthy stock from a good source. Plant them during the dormant season, spacing the bushes 1.2–1.5 m. (4–5 ft.) apart. This time do not deep plant but keep the root system at the same level as previously. Initial pruning should aim for an open, goblet-shaped bush with a clear stem at the base, so cut out any low branches. Remove about a third of the tips of the remaining shoots, leaving an outward-facing bud at the top of each stem.

CULTIVATION—Weed control, feeding, mulching, and watering in dry weather are all routine matters, similar to other soft fruits

PRUNING—Although liking similar conditions to blackcurrants, redcurrants, and white currants are pruned and trained in an entirely different manner. Redcurrants and white currants retain a framework of branches permanently throughout their lives. You can, therefore, train these as bushes or sometimes as cordons or standards. Cordons are treated like a single-stem bush, spur pruning all side shoots each year, and standards are treated like a bush on a leg. During future years aim to keep the center of the bush open and new growth directed to the sides. Fruit is produced on small side shoots called spurs. Side shoots should be reduced to one or two buds to encourage spur formation. In later years, complex spurs will need thinning.

HARVESTING—This can be a fiddly job due to the small size of the fruit. Wait till the majority of fruits are ripe and then pick the entire strig, possibly using scissors. Strip the fruit from the strigs using a fork.

RECOMMENDED RED AND WHITE CURRANTS
"Red Lake" AGM—*reliable, moderately vigorous, heavy crops, good flavor*
"Junifer"—*newish introduction, early ripening, good disease resistance*
"White Versailles"—*traditional variety but still good, sweet, reliable*

PESTS AND DISEASES—Currants suffer from aphids, in particular currant blister aphid, which shows as raised red blotches. Aphids live underneath leaves and any spray must be directed there. Birds will eat not only the fruit but also the winter buds, too. Fruit may develop botrytis in damp summers and shoots may be infected with coral spot disease, which is a pink fungus that appears on dead shoots but can spread to live tissues.

Gooseberries

This traditional fruit used to be highly revered and was intensively grown for competition. It is mainly used for cooking, although it can be very succulent when fully ripe.

CULTURE AND PRUNING—Treat them very much like redcurrants. They can be trained as bushes, standards or cordons. As the stems bear vicious spines, it is particularly important to aim for an open shape when pruning to allow for easy access to the fruit when picking.

HARVESTING—Immature fruits can be harvested for cooking or a proportion of the fruit left to fully ripen for eating fresh. Like all soft fruits, they must be protected from birds when ripening.

RECOMMENDED GOOSEBERRIE'
"Careless" AGM—*traditional variety, heavy cropping, good for cooking or jamming*
"Whinham's Industry"—*ruby red dessert fruit, good flavor, vigorous*
"Invicta" AGM—*relatively new, high yields, mildew resistant, mainly cooking use*
"Pax"—*red dessert fruit, exceptional flavor, mildew resistant, almost spine free*

PESTS AND DISEASES—Birds can be particularly damaging to the buds in winter and mildew can devastate the foliage in summer. Sawfly larvae are like small caterpillars and will feed on the foliage until it is totally skeletonised, if not controlled. Growing soft fruit in a netted cage can be counter-productive here as birds which would eat the caterpillars are excluded.

Rhubarb

As it's prepared as a sweet dessert, rhubarb is usually classed with fruits but it is the thick, succulent stems that are being produced. This is a permanent crop that takes a few years to reach peak cropping and then will yield for five to ten years. It is worth buying good, named varieties, rather than seedlings, to get a good crop.

CULTIVATION—Rhubarb should be planted in the winter using dormant crowns or in the spring with pot-grown plants. Prepare the soil in the normal way and plant 90 cm. (3 ft.) apart both ways. Water and feed regularly to build up a good strong plant for future years. Remove any stems that show signs of flowers.

Rhubarb can be left to grow normally for an early summer crop or you can cover crowns with an upturned bucket and pack round with straw to force for an early spring crop. Do not force newly planted crops or force the same plants two years running.

HARVESTING—Available mid-spring to early summer. When harvesting, never remove all the leaves and stop picking by mid-summer to allow the plants to build up strength for the next year. Remember, the green leaves are poisonous, so only the red stems can be eaten.

RECOMMENDED RHUBARB
"Champagne"—*deep red stems, early, good for forcing*
"Timperley Early" AGM—*good for forcing, thin stalks, sharp flavor*
"Stockbridge Arrow"—*dark red color, thick stems, heavy cropping*

PESTS AND DISEASES—Rhubarb is generally trouble free, although older crowns can suffer from crown rot. Dig out and destroy infected clumps.

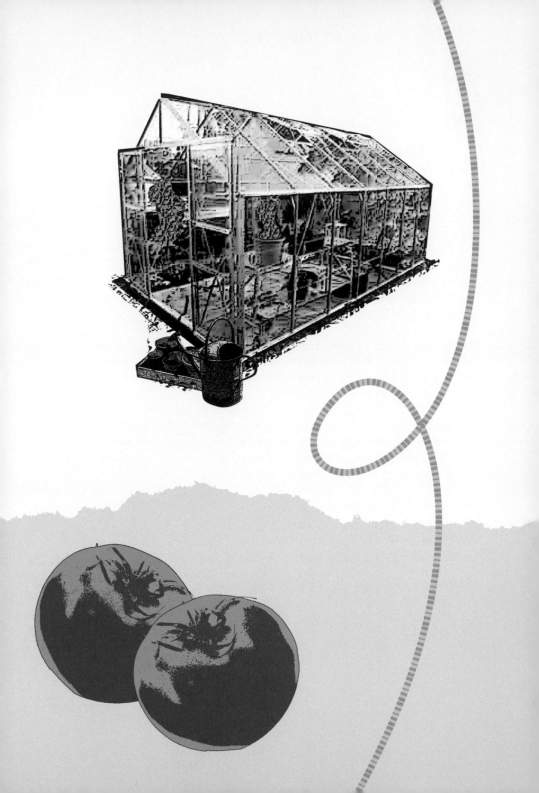

Greenhouses and polythene tunnels

Greenhouses and polythene tunnels are valuable additions to fruit and vegetable plots. Here you can raise your own vegetable plants and produce early or out-of-season crops. You can also achieve crops of tender vegetables, such as tomatoes and cucumbers, and can grow early strawberries, peaches, org grapes. There is also the joy of being able to garden in comfort, when the weather outside is awful!

Polytunnels

These are undoubtedly a cheap means of providing protection. They are made from hoops of galvanized steel, linked together to make a semi-circular tunnel shape. A large sheet of polythene is stretched tightly over the whole structure and anchored in a trench in the ground. Choose a good strong tunnel, as wind can be a problem with flimsy structures. Always cover a polytunnel on a warm day, as the polythene will be soft and stretch tight across the frame. There are usually simple doors at one or both ends which also act as ventilation.

Polytunnels are useful for providing limited protection for crops such as tomatoes and strawberries or for producing vegetable plants in spring. They lose heat quickly in the winter and heat up excessively in the summer, so need managing carefully. The polythene will usually last for two to three seasons but will then need replacing. There is always the risk of tears, which easily happen, and then a freak gust of wind can rip the whole structure and remove the protection in a few minutes.

Greenhouses

Greenhouses are relatively inexpensive and much more useful and substantial than polythene tunnels. Buy as large a greenhouse as you can afford and fit into your garden—controlling the temperature is easier and you are bound to need the space as your interest develops. The smallest viable size is 1.8 x 2.4 m. (6 x 8 ft.).

In the past, glasshouses were glazed with horticultural glass, which was cheap but fragile. For domestic purposes, particularly where there are children, it is worth getting toughened glass. Acrylic sheets are also possible but do not allow as much light through.

A good greenhouse will have enough height
to stand up in, without the risk of
banging your head. The door should
be wide enough for access with a
wheelbarrow and it should be well
braced at the ends and corners to
withstand wind. In particular, it should
have adequate ventilation with
opening vents on both sides of the
roof and on the side walls. Autovent
openers are simple devices that will
open the vents automatically on a
warm day and are well worth the extra cost, particularly if
the greenhouse is sited on an allotment, rather than in your own garden.

Greenhouses must be sited in a sunny spot. Avoid a windy location, and
position so that the long side faces south. Siting near to the house will be of
value, particularly if you intend to make electricity and water connections.

Some greenhouses have prefabricated or integral bases and do not require
a permanent foundation. They must still be placed on a firm, level base.
Ideally a concrete and brick foundation is by far the best and will avoid the
structure shifting at a later stage. Most domestic greenhouses are relatively
easy to construct, although some suppliers will offer an erection service as
well. When handling glass always use stout leather gloves.

Heating a greenhouse

An unheated greenhouse does have some value in that it will enable you
to provide a little basic protection to plants and start crops such as salads
and brassicas a bit earlier but not much. The real advantage comes if you
install a simple heating system that enables you to keep your greenhouse
or polythene tunnel frost free. This may not be for the whole year but at
least for the spring months, when you are raising young plants.

Electric greenhouse heaters are possible and have the advantage of thermostatic control. Remember that all electrical installations should be done by a competent electrician, particularly in a greenhouse where there will be water in close proximity to electrical equipment. Kerosene heaters are cheap but they have no control and must be refuelled frequently. They can also release noxious fumes. Heaters run from bottled gas are an excellent option, not too expensive to run and will have some thermostatic control. You can even get a changeover valve, which operates with two bottles of gas so that when one runs out, the supply transfers to the second.

Greenhouse equipment

Some benching is always useful in a greenhouse, as it brings smaller plants closer to working height. The ground is always the coldest, so young plants are better above the ground. Ideally, benching should be removable so that you can grow a summer crop, such as tomatoes, at ground level. A potting bench where you can keep composts and pots is essential, although this may not be in the greenhouse but possibly in a nearby shed.

For raising seeds, particularly of tender species such as tomatoes, cucumbers, and sweetcorn, a small electric heated propagator is desirable. For those that do not have electricity in the greenhouse, it will be simpler to site such a propagator on a windowsill in the house and then transfer seedlings to the greenhouse when established.

A clean watering can will be needed, although where lots of plants are grown, it will be quicker to use a hose pipe with a rose. Under no circumstances should you use water from a water butt. This is almost always contaminated with various plant diseases. It is a fallacy that rainwater is always better! Clean pots, trays, composts, plant labels, a small dibber, and a garden sieve are the other basic requirements.

Greenhouse management

Looking after a greenhouse is fairly straightforward but it does require determination and regular care. Most outdoor crops can be left for a few days or even weeks without major problems but greenhouses require daily attention, throughout most of the year. Certain automatic features are possible but even they require monitoring and checking.

Managing a greenhouse is all about creating the ideal environment for the plants you are growing. Firstly, the temperature should be controlled as evenly as possible. This means making sure that heaters operate efficiently at night time and that ventilators are opened early on warm days. A closed greenhouse can get very hot, very quickly, early on a summer's day. Unheated greenhouses need particularly careful attention. A greenhouse traps the sun's heat so it is prudent to close the ventilators in late afternoon or early evening to trap a little of the sun's warmth.

In summer it is useful to shade a greenhouse to reduce excessively high temperatures. This can be done with purpose-made blinds, plastic mesh, or with a coating of a special greenhouse shading paint that can be washed off in the winter. Never use emulsion paint for this job as it remains permanently!

Humidity is also of importance and will depend on the crop you are growing. For example, cucumbers like to grow in a much damper atmosphere than tomatoes. Humidity is easily increased by damping down the floors of the greenhouse with a hose.

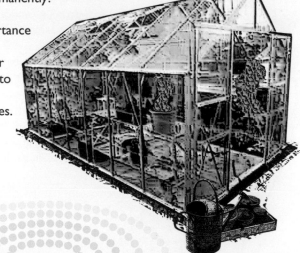

Damping down is also a useful means of cooling the greenhouse in very hot weather. In winter you should aim for a drier atmosphere by providing a crack of ventilation whenever the weather allows. This helps to avoid a build-up of humidity, which often results in diseases such as botrytis in winter lettuce.

Light is a vital consideration for plants and without adequate levels, plants cannot grow. So even if you heat a greenhouse in winter, plants will not grow unless there is enough light. This means that it is important to keep the greenhouse glass clean in winter to allow the maximum amount of sunshine to reach your plants.

Giving plants adequate water for growth, without drowning them, is also especially important in the greenhouse. In general, far more plants are killed by overwatering than underwatering. With plants in containers, you should always wait until the compost is looking or feeling dry and then give each pot a thorough soaking. This may need to be daily in midsummer but less than once a week in winter. Growbags in particular need very regular watering as the compost in these is shallow. Plastic rings are available which both increase the depth of compost in a growbag and help to direct the water. Hard and fast rules for watering cannot be given and you must check each plant to assess its water requirements.

Hygiene is very important in a greenhouse. Any pests or diseases spread rapidly in the enclosed atmosphere. Make sure all pots, trays, and equipment are thoroughly clean. Avoid storing things under the benches, as this inevitably becomes untidy and a hiding place for pests. Once a year, it is a good practice to thoroughly wash down the greenhouse inside and out, ideally using a horticultural disinfectant.

Plant production

Many vegetables benefit from being raised under glass before planting outside. A greenhouse gives greater control over conditions and plants can usually be started slightly earlier under glass giving a head start on cropping. The same basic procedures can be used for many vegetables.

Small seeds, such as lettuce, celery, tomatoes, and brassicas, should be sown in seed trays, gently covering the seed with a thin layer of sieved compost. Use a good seed or multipurpose compost. Cover the trays with glass and newspaper or black polythene, and place in a suitable temperature. Tender plants, such as tomatoes, will require a heated propagator running at about 21°C (70°F). Hardier vegetables can be much cooler. Larger seeds, such as sweetcorn, zucchinis or cucumbers, can be sown individually, putting two seeds into a 9 cm. (3½ in.) pot of multipurpose or potting compost. Again, cover with black polythene and germinate at about 21°C (70°F). Check daily, watering when needed and uncovering as soon as there are signs of germination.

The smaller seeds sown in trays will require pricking out into larger containers. You can use seed trays which will take 35 to 48 seedlings, multi-celled trays or individual small pots. Transfer the seedlings, holding the seed leaf only, and gently firm into their new location, watering in well. With those seeds that you have sown individually, remove the weaker seedling where both have germinated. Grow on young plants in light conditions at an appropriate temperature for the crop. Hardy vegetables, such as lettuce or brassicas, can be grown quite cool without any additional heat. Tender vegetables, such as tomatoes, zucchinis, sweetcorn, French beans. and cucumbers, will need to be kept at least frost free but ideally grown at about 12°C (55°F).

Greenhouse tomatoes

These are probably one of the most common but most rewarding vegetables to grow, although of course they are a fruit! Home grown tomatoes seem to have far more flavor than those bought from shops and are always welcome. There is a huge range of varieties available and as well as the familiar red ones, you can get yellow and purple types and various sizes from tiny currant-sized fruits, through to whopping slicing tomatoes. Growing in a greenhouse gives greater control over conditions and, therefore, an earlier and heavier crop.

Tomato plants can be obtained from any garden centre in the spring and early summer, but if you have a heated greenhouse, you can grow your own from seed. It is then easy to choose exactly which types you want to grow. You must be sure that adequate temperatures can be maintained.

SOWING AND PROPAGATION—Seed should be sown in early spring in a warm propagator at about 21°C (70°F) Prick out the seedlings as soon as the seed leaves have expanded, putting one seedling in a 9–10 cm. (3.½–4 in.) pot in a good potting compost. Keep the plants in a light area at a temperature of about 16°C (60°F). As they grow, space out the pots to avoid overcrowding. Plants are ready to move on when they are about 20–30 cm. (8–12 in.) tall and the first flowers are just showing.

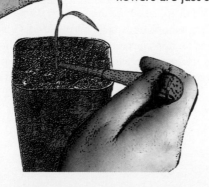

CULTIVATION—You can grow tomatoes in the border soil in the greenhouse if this has not happened previously but a build-up of pests and diseases rapidly occurs, so in future years, this will not be so successful. The alternative is to use large pots of potting compost, or growbags. These are laid flat and two or three holes are made in the top surface, into which tomatoes are planted. Holes must also be punctured in the base of the bag to create drainage. These are reasonably successful but they will need very frequent watering in hot weather, and heavy feeding.

If you are growing tomatoes in an unheated greenhouse, do not plant before late spring. If you are buying in plants, rather than growing your own, look for stocky, sturdy, smaller plants, rather than tall leggy ones. Space them out in the greenhouse to acclimatise for a few days before planting. The ideal temperature for growing tomatoes is around 16°C (60°F). Ventilate the greenhouse as necessary on warm days to avoid a build-up of high temperatures. If you are only growing tomatoes, do not use greenhouse shading, unless the summer is especially hot.

SUPPORT AND TRAINING—
Most greenhouse tomatoes are tall plants, correctly described as cordons, and will require support. Canes can be used in pots or border soil but these are more difficult in growbags. Alternatively, you can use strings tied to the greenhouse roof above the plants and dropped down to the plant. The lower end of the string is tied loosely around the base of the plant which is gently twisted around the string as it grows.

Greenhouse tomatoes are restricted to one stem, so all side shoots are removed as they appear. It is good to damp the plants over daily with water or lightly shake to encourage the dispersal of pollen and the pollination process. As soon as young tomatoes have formed, commence feeding regularly with a high-potassium tomato feed. As the fruit starts to ripen, the lower leaves are removed to allow light to reach the ripening fruit. This should only be done in moderation, as the leaves are vital for the plant's growth.

WATERING AND FEEDING—It is essential to water and feed tomatoes regularly. Water shortage will cause the young fruits to drop off or the development of blossom end rot, which is a physiological disorder showing as brown corky patches on the fruits. Yellowing between the leaf veins is a sign of magnesium deficiency, which often occurs with tomatoes. Use a dilute solution of Epsom salts, 20 g./lt. (2.5 oz./gall.) and water round the roots.

HARVESTING—Greenhouse tomatoes should be ready for picking from around early summer, depending on the sowing date and glasshouse temperatures.

RECOMMENDED TOMATOES
"Shirley" AGM—*an established variety, heavy crops, good in a cold greenhouse*
"Alicante" AGM—*another reliable variety, medium size, fine-flavored fruit*
"Vanessa" AGM—*vine-ripening type, fruit remains firm, sweet and juicy*
"Gardener's Delight" AGM—*heavy cropping, tangy, flavorsome cherry-sized fruit*
"Golden Sunrise" AGM—*golden yellow fruits with a very sweet flavor*

PESTS AND DISEASES—Tomatoes suffer from a bewildering range of pests and diseases, although most fortunately do not often occur. Whitefly is the greatest pest of tomatoes in a greenhouse. The best method of control is by means of the predator *Encarsia*. You may have to introduce this more than once in the season, as it is sometimes so successful that it often eradicates all whitefly and then dies itself. Some people also have success with marigolds planted around their tomatoes, which are strong-smelling and discourage the whitefly. Do this before the whitefly appear. If you decide to use chemical pesticides, you will need to spray frequently and there is then always the problem of the safe period between spraying and being able to eat the fruit.

Tomatoes also suffer from potato blight, which can devastate the crop and is impossible to control once it appears. If you are also growing potatoes, it is worth spraying the tomatoes at the same time as the potatoes, as a preventative measure. Viruses sometimes show as mottled, distorted leaves. Destroy plants before the virus spreads to others.

Grafted Plants

Recently, several retail seed merchants have started offering grafted totato plants by mail order. A fruiting variety of tomato is grafted onto a particularly strong-growing rootstock derived from a wild species. The result is a plant that is vigorous, resistant to root diseases and tolerant of low temperatures, providing early and heavy cropping. The union, the point where the plant was grafted, must stay above soil level. Grafted cucumbers, eggplants, melons, and peppers are also available with similar advantages.

Glasshouse cucumbers

Although small ridge cucumbers can be grown outside, a greenhouse is needed to produce the long, thin, traditional cucumbers. It is, of course, another fruit but treated as a vegetable, as it is eaten with savory dishes. Ideally, cucumbers require slightly different conditions to tomatoes but if you want just a few fruits, you can try a couple of plants in the same greenhouse.

SOWING—Seed should be sown in early spring in a warm propagator at about 25°C (78°F). Individual seed should be placed in 75 mm. (3 in.) pots of potting compost. Young plants must be grown on at a temperature of around 21°C (70°F). Don't overwater.

CULTIVATION—Cucumbers can be grown in growbags or the border soil. Ideally, a special raised bed is constructed utilizing old, well-rotted farmyard manure, topped off with good topsoil or potting compost. Such a root run will give excellent drainage and perfect conditions for establishing growth.

Train cucumbers as single stem plants, known as cordons. Tie to a 2.5 m. (8 ft.) bamboo cane or train up strings like tomatoes. As the side shoots grow, reduce them back to two or three leaves. During warm weather, water cucumbers frequently and feed regularly. Cucumbers like high humidity so the area around them should be damped down daily.

HARVESTING—Greenhouse cucumbers are usually available for picking by early to mid-summer.

RECOMMENDED CUCUMBERS

Choose all female varieties to avoid fertilized fruits, which are bitter.

"Femspot" Fi—*all female, high yielding, disease resistant*

"Landora" Fi—*all female, early crops, performs well in cooler conditions*

"Socrates" AGM and "Mini Munch" AGM— *both mini lunchbox cucumbers*

PESTS AND DISEASES Cucumbers are very prone to aphids, whitefly, red spider mite, and powdery mildew. The latter two are both deterred by ensuring a humid atmosphere. Red spider mite can be controlled by the predator *Phytoseilus*. Mildew requires the use of a fungicide, although there are some mildew-resistant varieties worth growing. Cucumbers are also prone to infection by virus diseases, which show as stunted plants with mottled yellowing leaves. This is easily spread to other plants so any showing virus symptoms should be removed and destroyed immediately.

Using Straw Bales

This alternative to growbags used to be very popular with commercial growers but is still quite valid for amateurs. It is particularly useful where crops, such as cucumbers or tomatoes, cannot be grown in the greenhouse soil because of diseases. You need traditional straw bales. Place them in the location where you want to use them because they will become very heavy when wet. Soak the bales thoroughly over a period of several days. Sprinkle some granular fertilizer, such as Growmore, onto the surface. The combination of moisture and nitrogen from the fertilizer will start the bale gently decomposing. When you're ready to plant, create a small bed of potting compost on the top and plant into this area.

As the bale decays, it will heat up just like a compost heap, providing a nutritious and warm root run. Straw bales also hold a far greater quantity of water than growbags and so are ideal if you cannot check watering regularly. This technique is suitable for growing almost any type of crop but is probably most useful for plants such as cucumbers, melons, peppers, and tomatoes.

Suppliers

Vegetable Seed Suppliers

American Seed Company
www.americanseedco.com

Rispens Seeds Inc.
www.rispensseeds.com

American Meadows
www.americanmeadows.com

Asgrow and Dekalb
www.asgrowanddekalb.com

Seeds by Design
www.seedsbydesign.com

Fruit Suppliers

Raintree Nursery
www.raintreenursery.com

Cummins Nursery
www.cumminsnursery.com

Johnson Nursery
www.johnsonnursery.com

C&O Nursery
www.c-onursery.com

Pest control

National Pest Management Association
A comprehensive resource for information
on pests
www.pestworld.org

Index